"*The Girl Got Up* is a powerful and honest book that weaves together spiritual journey and scriptural reflection. Rachel Srubas writes luminous and compelling prose. Once you begin reading, this book is very difficult to put down."

Cynthia M. Campbell
President emerita,
McCormick Theological Seminary

"My first impression of *The Girl Got Up* is my lasting impression: Rachel Srubas is someone who can be trusted—trusted to tell a compelling story; trusted to guide the reader with wisdom and subtle humor; trusted to weave together Scripture, personal narrative, and self-reflection without glossing over hard or painful truths. Few books plumb the depths of faith, skepticism, and yearning with such naked grace. It will take your breath away."

MaryAnn McKibben Dana
Author of *Sabbath in the Suburbs*

"Srubas tells her story and the Gospel story in a way that speaks of a lifetime of conversion, confession, and redemption with a warm, accessible, and familiar voice. *The Girl Got Up* is a joy and an encouragement to those seeking a deeper faith."

Rev. Alex Hendrickson
Founding board member,
The Young Clergy Women Project

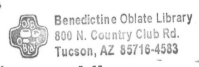

The Girl Got Up

A Cruciform Memoir

Rachel M. Srubas

LITURGICAL PRESS
Collegeville, Minnesota

www.litpress.org

Cover design by Ann Blattner. Cover photograph by Ed Snyder. www.StoneAngels.net.

Most of the poems in this work appeared previously in periodicals or anthologies, to whose editors the author expresses gratitude:

> "Wild Violet," "She Is the Breath," "Fatherland," and "Mother Tongue" appeared in *Spirit & Life*;

> "I Want to Marry You" appeared in *Another Chicago Magazine* and *The Best American Poetry 1992* (Collier Books, Macmillan Publishing Company);

> "A Bible Harlot" appeared in *Border Beat*;

> "Tomorrow, Tamar" and "Flocking" appeared in *Theology Today*;

> "Midrash for Hannah" and "Miriamic Hymn" appeared in *The Journal of Feminist Studies in Religion*.

Excerpt from "The Soul That Cries to God" by Jessica Powers from *The Selected Poetry of Jessica Powers*, published by ICS Publications, Washington, DC. All copyrights, Carmelite Monastery, Pewaukee, WI. Used with permission.

Scripture texts in this work are taken from the *New Revised Standard Version Bible* © 1989, Division of Christian Education of the National Council of the Churches of Christ in the United States of America. Used by permission. All rights reserved.

1	2	3	4	5	6	7	8	9

Library of Congress Cataloging-in-Publication Data

Srubas, Rachel M.
    The girl got up : a cruciform memoir / Rachel M. Srubas.
        p.   cm.
    Includes bibliographical references.
    ISBN 978-0-8146-3449-3 — ISBN 978-0-8146-3451-6 (ebook)
    1. Srubas, Rachel M.   2. Christian biography.   I. Title.
    BR1725.S725A3   2013
    285'.1092—dc23
    [B]   2012044172

For twelve apostles:

Rev. Susan Reggin
Rev. Rose C. Taul
Rev. Ann O. Johnson
Rev. Elizabeth Caldwell
+ Rev. Marguerite Bowden Reid
Sr. Lenora Black, OSB
Rev. Alexandra Hendrickson
+ Rev. Patricia Kilcullen
Sr. Diane Bridenbecker, OP
Rev. Rosanna Kazanjian
Rev. Sue Westfall
Ms. Lily Hendrickson

And He who redeems will use for the soul
the full extent of its cargo:
the songs, the memory's trivia, the sweet or acid tears,
the spoils or the debt of frightening arrears.
Ingenious to save, in the end His love
  will put to divine advantage
  the wisdom (if wisdom could be the word) of the wasted years.

Jessica Powers, "The Soul That Cries to God"

Contents

Prologue: Me and More: On Memoir and the Holy   ix

Chapter 1: Not Dead but Sleeping   1

Chapter 2: Whom Shall I Fear?   19

Chapter 3: Her Ways Wander   38

Chapter 4: Storied, Brief, and Sisterly   56

Chapter 5: The Word Was God   69

Chapter 6: Give Me This Water   89

Chapter 7: Bible Memory Helps   107

Acknowledgments   125

Me and More:
On Memoir and the Holy

Bookstores—the scarce, brick-and-mortar kind—now have prominent sections dedicated to memoir and autobiography. Might we suppose a correlation between an increasingly online culture and a plenitude of personal writing? As we spend more time in coolly virtual realms, are we getting hungrier for books that feel warm and confiding? Or does the connective, self-disclosive ethos of online social networks foster a readership especially hospitable to memoir? And what might be said about the holy in this context? When writers recount their experiments in biblical ethics and contemplative practices, their departures from church, sojourns in ashrams, or returns to religious tradition, readers buy up their books. While growing numbers of people in the United States claim no religious affiliation, many read memoirs of faith.

I appreciate the memoir trend. As a student writer in the 1980s and early 1990s, I had trouble inventing fictional plots. I wanted to write creatively without the make-believe hassle. But even at a university with an established degree-granting program in creative writing, there were no memoirists among the faculty and no classes in creative nonfiction. When such a class was eventually offered, more students showed up than there were chairs in the classroom to seat them. So I fueled myself with the energy of memoirs I admired, as well as the work of poets who drew on life experience. And I wrote on instinct.

About a year before I started writing this book, I participated in a writers' symposium. Several female spiritual memoirists were present. A respected man in the group cautiously hinted that a preponderance of women seemed to be writing about our personal lives and would do well to enlarge our vision and tackle topics beyond the autobiographical. I was both troubled and challenged by his remarks. How different were they from the criticism leveled at poet Anne Sexton when she wrote about her uterus? On the other hand, autobiographical writing, whether by men or women, is susceptible to narcissism and exhibitionism. I embarked on a research-heavy religious writing project that interested me to a point. But I found the conventional constraints of nonfiction and my chosen topic limiting my freedom to apply my writing to my life. Moreover, I was neglecting to mine my life experience for insight possibly relevant to readers. This omission seemed potentially to cheat them, and it made for rather anemic prose.

Then I received an email from Trish Sullivan Vanni at Liturgical Press. She said publisher Peter Dwyer "would like you to think about writing a book that ties to the women of the Bible in some way. Would you like to meditate on that, and see if an idea or two bubbles up?" I esteem that message as the best invitation to land in my inbox all year. Within hours of reading it, I had gently set aside my unfinished writing project and was imagining *The Girl Got Up*.

This is a book about me and more. "More" matters. There's arguably too much "me" in some memoirs, regardless of their authors' sex. Significantly, though, when women write memoirs we exercise autobiographical authority that in literary history we only very lately enjoy. Book buyers eagerly reading women's memoirs are making up for lost time and countless unwritten lives.

Add to this mix the lost times of church women, the centuries of unnamed women of faith with institutionally suppressed and prohibited vocations. I am a clergywoman and a preacher. I pastor a congregation in a denomination that for about sixty years has been ordaining women to serve as ministers of Word and Sacrament, yet I still strike some people as novel and exceptional. A woman who recently attended worship at my church said to me, "When I heard this church had a woman pastor, I said, 'Oh, no' because I've never had one before. But I'm glad I gave you a chance."

This book tells the story of my development from a girl without God to a woman of faith given the chance to serve as a pastor. Integral to the story I tell here are biblical narratives and verses, several of which are incorporated into the body of the book. I purposely mix biblical passages with my own writing because I mean to demonstrate my belief that people are called to enter into Scripture and let it mess graciously with us. Were it not for Scripture's women and Scriptures meaningful to me as a woman, I would practice neither faith in the God of grace nor ministry for God's sake.

The story I tell in this book is both personal and comparable to other women's (often unwritten) stories of spiritual development and religious calling. Present-day women's struggles, our ordinary times, and our victories resemble those of women in the Old and New Testaments despite great differences between their times and ours. Our life stories serve as lenses through which we read Scripture.

When women read the Bible, we can find in it much misogyny to discourage us. Some women understandably stop reading and look elsewhere for sacred teachings free of the anti-woman strains undeniably present in Hebrew and Christian Scriptures. Some women read on and find that these very Scriptures expose the ideological distortion of divine revelation. Without glossing over the subjugation and abuse of women the Bible frequently portrays, I ultimately find in it the Word of a wily, subversive, generative, and liberating God who raises up women and makes us strong in ways good for the world.

The Girl Got Up is not a Bible study, though my study of the Bible informs its pages. I am an intuitive writer. I like what poet Frank O'Hara said about writing: "You just go on your nerve." In all honesty, I presented to Trish Vanni an outline for this book's chapters, but then I departed from the outline because intuition, nerve, and the Holy Spirit led me differently, more deeply into the Bible and the writing experience than dutiful adherence to the outline would have allowed me. From the book's inception to its conclusion, I stayed true to my original purpose: to connect biblical women with present-day women by way of memoir. By granting myself the creative liberty to be guided by recollection, language, prayer, and the experience poet Robert Bly calls "associative leaping," I fulfilled my vision, if not my original outline, of a book about a girl who, with lots of holy help, finally got up.

Poets don't tend to outline before they write, and I was a poet long before I ever wrote a memoir. In this memoir I include some of my poems because they are intrinsic to my story, and they are inspired by biblical women. Besides, poetry is good and good for you, like dark chocolate and red wine.

This book is a tell-some, not a tell-all. It occupies the broad terrain between that permissive memoirist's axiom, *write as if everyone you know is dead,* and the mendacity that Sigmund Freud (in a 1929 letter to Edward Bernays) claimed "makes all autobiographies worthless." As a younger writer, I hurt a few people by writing as though they were dead (or as though I wished they were). That kind of writing is not brave; it's shortsighted and mean. Buddhists identify a virtue called "right speech," which certainly has a Christian cousin. Think of the New Testament Letter of James. It calls the tongue a fire. Speak to illuminate, not burn. Likewise, writing fingers are matches. Be careful where you strike. And what does "careful" mean for a memoirist of faith? It means be neither mean nor mendacious. It means speak the truth in love. Love rejoices in the truth. What is truth? That was Pontius Pilate's question. Yes, in this broad terrain lie a number of ethical hazards.

Nevertheless, I rejoice in telling in this book some truths I would not proclaim from the pulpit nor mention at Thanksgiving dinner. I rejoice in the big intimacy of spiritual memoir, the writing of which is surely prayer for me. Here the personal serves literary and devotional purposes not confined to my private life. My rendering of certain memories and my musings on selected Scriptures are not meant to interest you in me but to engage your mind in the spirited things that words biblical, autobiographical, theological, and poetic can do. I am not the words of this book, but I take full responsibility for those I have written and for my use of the Scriptures.

When I write about other people, I do so honestly, portraying my very partial perceptions of them, not making complete or objective presentations. I have changed some persons' names or left some persons unnamed. I have dealt truthfully, though by no means journalistically, with the reality that my coming to faith in God involved departing spiritually from my parents. The departure was hard, and the need for it was painful. It led me to greater health than I could otherwise have known. My faith has made me well. In this wellness I find it possible to love and honor my parents without pretense. Love rejoices in the truth. I rejoice in the cruciform life. I give thanks to God for the privilege of writing this book about how I came to live it.

August 28, 2012
Feast Day of Augustine of Hippo

1

Not Dead but Sleeping

Avocado green—that iconic color of the 1970s. A post-psychedelic, pre-punk color. It was the color of the boxy telephone mounted to the kitchen wall with its extra-long, slightly grimy coiled cord. The drapes hanging in the dining room were avocado green, as were the melamine summer dinner plates we would use on the back patio picnic table. The ceramic lids on the kitchen canisters, the tint in the chubby, faceted glass that made my milk look like the produce of an unwell cow—all varying versions of avocado green. An indecisive, disappointed, yet weirdly fashionable color at the time, even the glossy cardboard gift box tucked into the shelf in my bed's headboard bore two different shades of it, lighter on the bottom, deeper on the lid. That box, roughly the dimensions of a page-a-day calendar, held secrets darker and brighter to me than the pureed hue of their container.

Secrets were big because I was getting to be a big girl, and I had come to sense there was more to be

1

known than was told, more to wonder about than I felt free to ask. Watergate, whatever that was, seemed to be a secret the radio kept talking about but never quite revealing. I envisioned a gate holding back water. There were leaks, of course. Water, my favorite substance on earth, loved to run, but prevented from running, it would seep and stain. And then the secret would be out.

Maybe I was a secret. Maybe I was water they had hoped the gate would hold back, but I leaked and then I had to be admitted.

I would mope around the house, wearing hand-me-downs. I made a lot of noise, wanted lots of attention, and felt fundamentally unnoticed, or when noticed, largely disregarded. The members of my family were living their lives, and these family members comprised a system wherein the newest, smallest member, a female, could not readily attain notice except by being needy and disruptive. Thus I was annoying to others and secretly important to myself. Thus I became a writer.

A writer is a teller of secrets you didn't know you knew until you see them spelled out and feel that jolt of recognition. Or a writer is a technician, like my father, who wrote technical manuals concerning locomotives for a living. Or a writer is pray-er talking back to the Author of life. How like a writer to write about what a writer is. Readers have had a lot of that—writing by, for, and about the writer. Readers keep reading, though, because a writer can also be an upholder of mirrors, a shiner of lights, and a namer of names. People in general, and readers especially, are curious creatures and nosy.

The handsome president died. My mother's father died. A couple years later, I was born. My life is a gift despite having been hard early, in that way life can be hard for people who always have enough to eat, booster shots, warm if pre-worn clothes, and amusing toys. This book is a thank-offering that will get to the gratitude often by way of the woe that precedes the blessing, the turnabout way of Beatitudes. The honesty here is selective, impressionistic, incomplete, and intrinsically thankful even when the memories are hard. I am more interested in messy life written faithfully than in scrapbook sentiment rendered prettily. By faithfully I mean with unflinching fidelity to the search for holiness regardless of circumstance. Think of magi searching for the baby Christ birthed amid livestock and manure during a road trip, under the reign of a tyrant king. To God I give thanks for my own sanitized and safer birth.

Life is a gift we sometimes mistake for a prize. Humans are covetous beneficiaries. We lust for the life we're given. Whatever it took for me to be given my life, I am glad I am, and I want to keep being. The appetite for living and the resurrection faith that drive this book, and me, are forms of greedy devotion. I don't want mere life, I want life in God, and not just now, but forevermore.

The basement was finished and furnished. The basement stairs descended into a spacious multipurpose room where more living happened than happened in the living room upstairs. We never called the basement a rec room, though we could have. Enormous built-into-the-wall stereo speakers, their nubby fabric covers flecked with metallic thread, flanked a brick fireplace. LP records—Nat King Cole, George Carlin, Walter Schumann and The Voices of Christmas—crammed a bookcase. A sloping antique mantle clock on a stone shelf told the right time twice a day. The bulky television in the corner was inhabited by people made of light who busied themselves entertaining us at night. There was knitting done down here; woolen creations emerged from the long dance of my mother's needles. Here my father relaxed in the evening because he worked by day, like the clockwork of a clock that works, and by night, after supper, he needed to sit and take things in and not be bothered.

In a playroom on the opposite side of the basement, a round aluminum table stood in a corner beneath a shaded hanging lamp of a mod, ovoid shape. You could lift the padded seats on the benches surrounding the table and find they were full of games and art supplies. You could invent a whole world in this playroom, and I did, drawing chalk roads for matchbox cars on a threadbare rug. Between the playroom and the family room, a ping-pong table frequently bore the piled fabrics and flimsy paper patterns of my mother's sewing projects. Her pinking shears would drily munch through these, and sometimes my father would disappear into the Off Limits.

Deeper in the basement than the bar with its icebox full of Meister Brau, behind a pair of louvered doors, the unfinished Off Limits held mechanical dangers including a mangle for ironing bed sheets and a wringer I had been warned would mangle my foot if I didn't watch out. I wanted the Off Limits to warrant its foreboding name, but really, despite the laundry-related hazards and power hand tools hooked to a pegboard, it offered little intrigue. It was a space in which a woman and a man went about their grownup labor of cleaning and repairing the things we needed to make our way in the rest of the house, the rest of our lives. The Off Limits seemed to speak of little else than limits, especially its corner room. Windowless and scarcely larger than a closet, it no longer served its original purpose as my father's writing studio. Now it was my mother's sewing room. When you were in the playroom on the other side of the wall, you could hear the muffled intermittent electrical moan of her Singer machine as she pressed its foot pedal, fabricating a garment.

Never, I confess, never did I truly appreciate the clothes my mother skillfully sewed for me, and they were many—jumpers and slacks and smocks. Some weren't made for me in the first place, but for my sister, or even for my brother. They weren't what I would have chosen to wear. The life of a child, I was reminded daily, was a life of few choices. You got what you were given, and you did what you were told. Your aspirations and preferences were of little import or impact. So went the parenting style of the day, and of my parents in particular, who had effectively agreed that even my father's aspirations and preferences—his aspiration to write fiction in that tiny back basement room, his preference for science fiction in particular—would be set aside in favor of the home-manufacture of family attire. Domesticity, practicality, and the nimble industry of my mother's sewing hands prevailed over the imaginative urge of my father's writing mind. I know this about the sewing room's history because my sister (who for a teenage interval turned the sewing room into a bedroom in which to seek refuge from her prying little sister) learned of it and told me. I recall the avocado green feeling that came over me when I understood that my father had abandoned his literary potential.

Whom shall I blame?

Shall I blame my mother for neglecting to nurture my father's nascent literary dreams? Shall I blame my father for letting the workaday demands of career and household override the lonesome basement discipline of story craft? Or shall I just blame Meister Brau?

Why not, for all the good laying blame accomplishes? Meister Brau, Chicago's cheapest lager, the Ford Pinto of beers, jaundiced and dilute with a urine-forward flavor and slightly skunky finish, ensured my father's fiction never did get written.

Life with an alcoholic father can be fun. But you do have to seize your moments.

We were competitive swimmers, we three kids. At some point early in my brother's life, it was decided our childhoods would revolve around the pool—the indoor high school lap pool in the winter and the immense outdoor municipal pool in the summer. Somebody threw me into the water before I could walk. I could paddle with the best of them, and by age six, I was lining up on deck with the other drenched and stringy children, feeling vaguely superior to most because the strokes came easily to me. By age eight, I was on the team, winning events for my age group.

My father would pick me up from evening swim team practice. I would walk the empty halls of the high school, my hair lank and chlorinated, step outside into the dark, and spot the brown Chevy idling under the parking lot's sodium lights. My dad would let me play with the radio dials for the short drive home. Keith Richards, according to the Rolling Stones' hit single "Happy," did not want to live like his father, working for the boss every night and day. Melodiously bellowing on the car radio, Keith needed a love to make him happy, and really, who didn't? Sometimes my father let me steer the car on Highway 83, and I loved the heavy gliding feel of the big driving machine. Adjusting the steering wheel really did turn the car.

"Can I drive tonight?" I once asked.

"Not tonight."

"You let me last night."

"I was drunk."

And that settled it, somehow. The rules could change and change back just like that. The fun could come and go at whim, and when it went, something somber took its place, something silent I glumly understood I was not to disturb.

I dove into the water and loved the breathless immersion-blue silence. I wished I could stay down longer, wearing my goggles, gliding beneath the hollering surface of things. But in the end I always had to burst upward for breath.

I developed an interior life known to no one but me, an underwater sensibility I could put into effect even when I was bone dry and everyone including me was talking and walking around. Swimming through my life, especially my home life, meant the voices were muffled, the images blurred, and my pulse thumped an unremitting drumbeat inside me. It's not how you want a child with innately exploratory gifts and sensory attunement to have to live. But it was a fluid coping skill that provided me with a portable, use-anywhere refuge from people accustomed to telling me you're a nuisance, go play. Play tends to be serious business for kids, often less about fun and games than about learning to function gamely in a win-lose system. To swim as I swam, in competitive races, or underwater in the deep end, or in the drifting aquamarine consciousness behind a mental watergate, is to play alone, and I played alone very well.

It's not that I was unloved. I was loved. I enjoyed a sometimes enchanted little girlhood, picking wild violets for my mother on the walk home from school. During summer vacations, I helped to pitch the big green canvas tent in the woods where we five would sleep in lumpy bags warmed by campfire-heated rocks. My fondest childhood memory is surely of my father on camping trips, rising earlier than the rest of us to fry bacon and brew coffee that smelled wonderful. My father was a steadfast provider and capable cook who in later years mastered paella and lemon-roast chicken, bringing to the kitchen the same deft sensibility that characterized his home repair projects.

The brightest years of my father's life took place, I believe, before I turned ten, when my mother started working jobs outside our home. That summer my father suffered a heart attack, in the cause of which alcohol likely figured. After he came home from the hospital, we ate whitefish more often than hamburger, and I was supposed to be very quiet.

As chlorine bleaches pool water and kills the human microbes that would fester in it, alcohol thins familial blood and kills the human goodness that would flourish in it. Alcoholism sterilizes love, renders it incapable of fruitful reproduction. The alcoholic family soaks in the chill juice of its once-glad, now-captive spirit. The alcoholic goes from enjoying a beer to stashing vodka to chase a thousand beers, and the chase is never-ending, never rewarded. The drunk's relations join in, chasing after normalcy, which has taken its leave. Pretense takes normalcy's place. Everyone pastes on a publicly passable face. Everyone comes home from school or work or the grocery store or the pool and navigates the evening, performing as if everything's okay and a smug, destructive demon is not really squatting in the middle of the household. The family's performances include acts of love, and the actors were born to play these roles. *Good night*, they tell each other, and they mean it. *Good night, John Boy!* they joke. *Sleep tight!* And the lights go down, and everybody sleeps except the demon.

That is, most everybody sleeps, most nights. I underwent a bout of childhood insomnia. But was it really a bout? Or was it a single sleepless night? And was it the whole night, or one long fidgety stretch of dark hours I never wanted to live through again? Memoir and gospel readers, take note: what memory cannot fully recall, imagination will supply. In fourth grade I discovered the power of imagination at play with words. Having written several short stories that won me paper-and-glitter badges announcing "I Am A Creative Writer!" I felt the first of the vocational urges toward the writing life that this book evidences I still feel. Whereas my childhood stories were fantastic invented adventure tales that granted me a reprieve from reality, some parts of this book revisit real scenes I wanted to escape when they occurred. Other parts recollect memories I would like to preserve. In either case, I mean to retrieve and revive the girl who often did her best to submerge or sleep through the parts of life that hurt.

Wild Violet

Early March, my Midwestern childhood
marches to the forefront of my memories.
Lord, the everlasting school year
and the never-coming summer.
I would scrape my small bootsoles
along Maple Street's curb,
searching the dirt for life signs—
a faint, chartreuse shoot, or—could it be?
a wild violet? I would drop to my knees
for just one. Its unfolding purple symmetry
meant everything to me. No matter
that the soil's persistent winter cold crept
into my flesh and my unfinished bones.

A wild violet was a secret
that gave itself away—hinting
something more
was preparing to spring forth:

a naked and unreasoned season,
artful, earth-scented and defiant, with power
to remake the world, awaken you, too,
and even resuscitate and recreate me—
a prayerless girl with soiled knees
and a stubborn, long-hibernating heart.

Something prompted me to hide a couple grownup sleeping pills in the avocado green treasure box I kept on the shelf in my bed's headboard. I recall the baby blue toilet tissue the tablets were wrapped in more clearly than I recall my reason for stealing them from my parents' medicine chest. One night, sick in bed with some respiratory infection, I swallowed them and told no one. The next day, my mother shook me awake. Her eyes looked round and alert. A peculiar afternoon-tinged daylight shone at the edges of the shaded bedroom window. I learned it was after four o'clock. The pills had worked. I had slept for more than sixteen hours and had not, apparently, shown any probability of waking up soon on my own. I was groggily surprised that my mother, who liked me quiet, had roused me. That's a child's logic for you: *I thought you liked me quiet.* A parent's logic finally says, *My God, what's wrong with my kid?*

They borrow power from God, parents do—power to give a child life. As soon as she's birthed and home, still luminescent with amniotic mystery, the power recedes, and something else takes its place. Parental skills kick in, or instincts or good sense or trial-and-error inventiveness or terror and learning and luck kick in, or some combination of all these, but not what you would readily call power. Parents are powerless before their powerless children. No one knew this better than the leader of the synagogue who came and knelt before Jesus.

> While he was saying these things to them, suddenly a leader of the synagogue came in and knelt before him, saying, "My daughter has just died; but come and lay your hand on her, and she will live." And Jesus got up and followed him, with his disciples. Then suddenly a woman who had been suffering from hemorrhages for twelve years came up behind him and touched the fringe of his cloak, for she said to herself, "If I only touch his cloak, I will be made well." Jesus turned, and seeing her he said, "Take heart, daughter; your faith has made you well." And instantly the woman was made well. When Jesus came to the leader's house and saw the flute players and the crowd making a commotion, he said, "Go away; for the girl is not dead but sleeping." And they laughed at him. But when the crowd had been put outside, he went in and took her by the hand, and the girl got up. And the report of this spread throughout that district. (Matt 9:18-26)

In this desperate, disruptive scenario, the man is a leader of nothing, not even his own life. He ricochets from his daughter's deathbed to crumple at the feet of a wandering miracle worker who talks in riddle-sequences of wedding feasts and old cloaks and new wine. Nothing in the father's synagogue religion, nothing of his ritual office, suits him for this crisis or prepares him for the plea he hears himself making. Despite what they say about girls and women, his daughter is his temple. Light shines through her that reveals the holy in the world. If she is dead, God may as well be. If God is God, this Jesus may as well be the Messiah. The father of the girl bets everything on Jesus—his honor, his faith—groveling like a beggar, purity and dignity be damned. I wonder, to this day I wonder, what it would be like to have a father capable of this.

The sick girl's mother makes no appearance in the story, unless the hemorrhaging woman whose story frames the girl's is her mother. What ails the girl? Is she bleeding too? Could it be that she, having learned to her prepubescent horror that growing up female entails bloodshed, decided with a theatrical flourish that she would rather die than get her period? Given my own menstrual introduction, such an unorthodox reading of the story seems not too far-fetched.

When I was thirteen years of age, there came a week when my mother was suddenly hospitalized. For reasons unclear to me at the time, her blood had to be transfused with that of donors. While she was in the hospital, my first period came. On my own I had to learn my way around tampons and pads. Furious that she would abandon me on the momentous occasion of my first period, startled that menstrual blood in fact *flowed* more heavily than that from, say, a skinned knee, I telephoned my mother's hospital room and yelled at her, "I don't *like* this. I don't want to *do* this," as though I had a choice. I recall a weary gentleness about her voice coming through the phone, telling me she would be home soon.

In the gospel the hemorrhaging woman's story bleeds into that of the helpless synagogue leader and his daughter. The woman is made well even while the dirging mourners blow and wail their songs for the dead girl. The curious cluster and gawk around the synagogue leader's home. Jesus dispatches them, claiming the man's daughter is not dead but sleeping. Undeterred by the jeers, Jesus is mad with Spirit, but quiet, and his gestures are not extravagant. There is no magic about him, no fanfare or tricks. He employs his proximity, his presence and his hands, his greed for more life than his own to pass through them, his disgust with death. He avails himself completely to the moment and its homely need, and thus, the girl gets up. She gets up and lives. Her panicked father and his beautiful cultic traditions hint at salvation, but they cannot do the job. Deep down everybody knows this and counts on it. Mourning is a way of life for people whose religion mostly perfumes and ritualizes human powerlessness and loss.

We cannot do the jobs that need to be done, it turns out. We cannot wake ourselves up, or stanch our blood, or save our kids, or lead our people by any power vested in us because none is. We do not parent on our own power, or protect our children, or grow from children into adults, or grow adults into disciples of Jesus on our own power. We are bodies, believers, doubters, and daughters, drinkers and drivers and swimmers and sleepers, and we are blood temples through which mercy not of our own concocting courses. We live—I know I live—only at the mercy of mercy. The girl got up in mercy and lived on power not her own and not even Jesus' own. He was a vagrant bumming power from God. He was the butt of jokes until his became the name on everybody's hungry lips. He was a wanted man, then, which is not to say he was loved.

I needed love to make me happy, but the love I got often made me lonely. That's the problem with broken love, drunk love, and baffled love. It leaves you wondering if no love at all would be better (it wouldn't be), if sleeping your life away would be preferable to living it semi-conscious that something is missing, something is wrong.

I did my best to love my family and became industrious about doing so during Advent. I would craft Christmas gifts for my parents and siblings from cigar boxes, discarded Christmas cards sent to us in years past, glue, yarn, and the like. We did not observe Advent as the season of hopeful expectation of Christ's coming, nor even have a countdown calendar with chocolates hidden behind the numbered days, but Christmas was important to work up to. Christmas can be very important to families that do not believe in Christ, as my family did not, who believe only in the private pajama ritual of presents. For Christless families that practice no religion at all, much rides on the familial living room gathering, the giving and receiving of gifts. There is no other wintry tradition to observe, no myth to recount, no candles to light in sequence, no community with which to pray about the deeper meaning of this day, no needy neighbors to receive the overflow of our bounty. There were, of course, poor families even in our generally affluent suburb of Chicago, and there were certainly churches in town. Our Scout troops assembled in their basements on weekdays after school. But the deeper meaning of this day was a faith that had died with my forebears. Now ours was a postwar, white flight, baby boom, secular home almost entirely devoid of ancestral customs. We replaced faith with the funnies on Sundays, and family traditions with forgetting and secrets.

Good news of even the most domestic sort, like that of Jesus giving life back to a little dead girl, will travel throughout a community and become its pride—*and the report of this spread throughout that district.* But when evil prevails, people dissemble and disassociate, forget and keep secrets. Even if the story of evil gets out, it is shrouded in shame and disowned by denial.

Take for example my mother's father and the evil he escaped. The story of it haunted him, or so I have gleaned from my mother's limited and rarely retold memories. Ashamed that in 1915 God had allowed the extermination of his closest relations and many other Armenians of Turkey, my grandfather immigrated to the United States and put his ancient Christian faith to death. He divorced himself from the once-great Armenian Orthodox Church whose every liturgy in the wake of the massacres must have seemed hopelessly funereal. He denied he needed God and denied the possibility that God would lift a finger to help the helpless.

To survive genocide is ghastly good fortune. You cannot help but bequeath burdened blood to your kid. My grandfather's only daughter received no resurrection report, not from her father and not, it would seem, from her mother. As an adult, my mother could not convey good news to her children. On Christmas Day, we three kids received our gifts like happy clueless magi under a starless sky. Our parents busied themselves, stoking the festive fire, studding with garlic cloves that vestige of the Armenians, the leg of lamb that would be our roast holiday dinner. But Christ was not born at our house. Merrily we would sit around the Christmas afternoon TV and blaspheme the beer commercial: "Pure-brewed in *Clod's* Country!"

The faith of my father had been that of his parents—a butcher and a chamber maid, Catholic Lithuanian immigrants. If my father took his inherited religion overseas with him as a young enlisted man, he did not bring it back with him from the war in Europe. There he may have seen and done terrible things for his country, I cannot say for certain. As a child I once asked him, "Do you believe in hell?" A taciturn veteran to say the least, he replied, "You create your own hell here on earth." And why would a thoroughly unchurched child ask her father if he believed in hell? It seemed a safer question than the one I really wanted to ask: Do you believe in God?

God was "Clod" in our family, religion an object of ridicule on the occasions when it came up at all, which were as infrequent as our conversations about the Armenian genocide or about my father's experience of combat. To a large extent, twentieth-century trauma made us who we were. You name it—genocide, immigration, urban poverty, world war, their mothers' early deaths—by the time in the 1950s that the man and woman who would become my parents met, all of these had traumatized them. They were one of ten couples who married in a single year while working in the offices of a defense department contractor that transported hydrogen bombs.

Soon after the wedding, my mother quit her job, my father got a better one, and the two made an ethnically indistinct white family in a ranch style house in the expanding suburbs of Chicago. The times were prosperous, but trauma lived with the family like an uninvited relative who camps on the couch. Trauma kept my mother in the frequent headaches and wretched moods that dominate my childhood memories of her. Trauma kept the icebox (that's what my father, born in the 1920s, always called the refrigerator) stocked with beer by no means brewed in God's country.

It was to such a world as ours that the Messiah came. Change a few of my story's historical details, and you've got the world in sin and error pining into which Jesus was born amid bleating beasts, to a couple doing their frightened best to manage. Wherever people scrape and clamor to salvage their lives and fashion their families, wherever women bleed for a dozen years and men are desperate for help with their unreachable daughters, there is Jesus, perennially employed. While the details of the stories change, the essential paradoxes persist. People are powerless and scared. People need love to make them happy. God permits our suffering. Yet God is with us and God is good.

I dimly sensed the human side of these realities when I was little, getting to be a big girl. The radio grownups clearly had no power to close the Watergate. The water of our lives rose and receded and tossed us around and submerged us and seeped, and we could swim or we could drown, but we could never make the water go away. It was like the deep stuff over which the first wind ever blew, and you attempted to levee it at your peril. You made friends with it if you could, as Chicago made friends with the Great Lake Michigan that curved and lapped at the city's eastern edges and spread out cold and lively toward the horizon.

When Chicagoland, as they call it, is the only world in which you've ever lived, you don't realize the sky over other places is not whitish and opaque in quite the same way it often is over Chicagoland. Its sky is frequently a thick and low presence, not a clear blue upward sweep toward the sun. Darken the pale skyline with the crush and concentration of urban architecture, much of it plainly functional, boxy and stacked, and you live in a corridor, under a cloud.

This cloud visited me when I was home alone on a school day morning. My father had left for work, my brother for high school, and my mother had driven my sister to junior high. I was wearing a hand-me-down quilted bathrobe with too-long sleeves, doing my assigned chore of washing breakfast dishes. The great, invisible, and speechless life that hid inside the white sky made itself known to me. The cloud entered the kitchen and confronted me, not tangibly, but truly. I was thunderstruck, breathless, noticed and accounted for as I had never before been seen or known. I knew my name, Rachel, and I loved its two irreducible syllables. It meant *lamb*, and I warranted it, somehow, in all its tender and Hebraic connotation. I had lived my few years housed and parented yet lost and unshepherded, but now, inexplicably, I was found.

The Lord cries "Samuel!" and eventually Samuel hears. The psalmist knows full well his days were inscribed in God's book before he was born to write poems. Gabriel shows up at Mary's house, and she rightly questions his claims before she consents to conceive with the Spirit. What are these stories but prequels to our own, and who are these people but people like us? Yes, in the guise of a gray midwestern morning, in a thunderous, cumulous silence I heard in my temples, God drew near to me in my bathrobe, the vestment of a thoroughly unprepared postulant, and dipped my hands into dishwater made abruptly holy.

I told no one about the fearsome, wondrous kitchen encounter, which ended the moment I heard my mother coming home through the front door. What citizen of Clod's Country could I possibly have told?

Soon afterward, while crafting Christmas presents for my family at the table in the corner of the playroom, I came upon a discarded greeting card an acquaintance had once sent to my parents. It bore a lush illustration of an open book. In raised golden script on the book's pages a message began "Our Father." I was pretty sure it was a big, famous prayer, something people said by heart. I knew better than to glue it to any of the gift collages I was making for my family. And I didn't want to share it, anyway. I wanted the prayer for myself. I used my safety scissors to cut it out, and it became a holy card. Its forbidden language of devotion addressed a parent greater than any other.

That the prayer's addressee was the same presence that had seized my awareness at the kitchen sink was not something I considered. I was still a little kid, making my way in a world not yet depleted of all beauty by quiet despair or common sense. I simply acted on instinct and slipped the prayer card into the avocado green treasure box that had previously held the purloined sleeping pills. I figured a kid was entitled to a few secrets. Because she loved me, because I was her child, my mother tucked me in at night and kissed me. Her face would come near the box that held the prayer, but she didn't know it was in there, and I dared not tell her. In secret, after my mother had bid me sweet dreams, I worked at memorizing the Our Father, then slipped off to sleep, hoping to wake up a better girl.

2

Whom Shall I Fear?

Our Father didn't answer.

Now a voice of pious rationality would like to have its say: *Of course God answered your prayers, just not in ways you could understand yet as a child. You understood it better by and by.*

I could write a book that looks back and says, *There, there. See! God is good. Jesus loves the little children.* I could write a feel-good book with "Heaven" in its title. To the best of my ability to tell, when I was a little child, Our Father who art in heaven did not hear my prayers, much less answer them. A kid says, *Hello! Anybody home!* and gets silence in return enough times, she finally concludes the house is empty.

To my young self, Our Father's silence sounded uncannily like my dad's. If he once had had more to say for himself, poverty, combat, and booze, family life and heart disease had drummed the speech out of him. By contrast, my mother's voice rang around

19

our family, wordy and emphatic as the prayers I whispered
urgently at bedtime, until at last I wised up, and like my
father who pretty much quit talking, I quit praying.

Our Father in heaven was a silence to be left unbroken.
Speak to it and I would be talking to myself until another
voice, not of heaven, cut me in the ear, telling me what was
what. My parentage, male and mute, female and vociferous,
had driven me to prayer. But my parents could not teach
me how to pray or how to trust the silent God about whom
they both apparently had deep if unacknowledged misgiv-
ings. It was best, my mother and father had decided, to busy
themselves with the obligations of providing and homemaking—never mind that these very occupations could be seen
as metaphors for God's own providence and nurture. The
trouble was, God's spacious sovereignty allowed people freedom to do what they would, which could include making
their own hell on earth and making life hell for others. Who
needs a permissive, unhelpful deity like that? And who has
time for religion when you've got these kids to raise, this job
to do between one war and the inevitable next?

I needed faith as a kid. I needed to love the God I knew
was hidden in the snow-colored sky. I needed to learn a moral
pattern and live it in a community more promising than our
quietly unwell family of five. Alcoholism and all that attends
it in a household—evil spirits—were doing their demonic
number on us. We were becoming cold, discrete as the ice
cubes suspended in a stiff drink. I had encountered other
families that seemed warmer and more unified than ours. I
sometimes slept over at friends' houses. In safe and private
moments, I would ask them what Sunday school was like.
But I knew better than to think my family would ever trundle
off to church together. I knew better than to violate our tacit
taboo by asking why we never would.

Besides, in our America, Christendom's tall steeples had
started faintly wobbling from the seismic cultural shifts of

the mid-to-late twentieth century. By the time of my young years in the late 1960s and early 1970s, at least in some regions of the country, parents could choose with impunity not to practice or impose on their children religious beliefs they did not sincerely hold. My parents, unlike those who sent their kids to Sunday school without attending worship themselves, are at least to be admired for the integrity of their functional atheism. We ate pancakes on Sunday mornings and read nothing holier than the funnies. In adulthood I have not had to unlearn bad, inherited religion, and this, I think, is no small blessing.

I have met numerous women for whom religion in childhood consisted chiefly of a shaming, sin-centered catechesis. Years later some still struggle to find their way to a life-giving theology and spirituality. Their childhood prayers were obligations they performed like chores, and chants they repeated after their Sunday school teachers, almost exclusively women, who may never have learned it was possible to have a relationship with God and not merely a religion about God.

I had no religion to teach me to wait on the Lord until the relationship could blossom in good time. Into my being, the silence of Our Father and my father, the noisy chastisements of my mother, carved a message I had lots of time to try to decode. What I lacked were deciphering tools, whatever they might have been. I did what a kid knows how to do. I made it all my fault. I blamed myself for being the family's and even the world's unwelcome misfit. With a child's self-centered grandiosity, I believed I was utterly unlovable. The only course I knew to follow, then, was the self-loathing way toward womanhood that many girls travel. I might come off looking good at times; I might be a bright, articulate, and physically healthy girl. But there would be more—or I should say less—to my story.

When I was a little girl, I had a nightmare as black and white and frantic as the opening scenes of *The Wizard of Oz*.

The twister in question was not a tornado but my mother, incoherent, spinning in her apron while every appliance in the kitchen whirred and smoked. For reasons having as much to do with the everyday demands of childrearing as with her nervous temperament, my mother rarely paused to take a breath or a break, and never to my knowledge paused to pray. While my mother was laundering my diapers, minding my preschool-age sister, enrolling my brother in kindergarten, and packing my father's lunches, second-wave feminists were setting out to liberate women. My mother whirred and smoked, getting family meals on the table, outfits sewn (soon to be outgrown), and kids to school or pool, a mentholated Benson & Hedges ever clamped between her lips. When I was still little, in the same kitchen where my mother huffed and seared and wiped and stewed, I stood at that sink of dishwater. Unbidden, a great power seized my awareness. I ascertained briefly the dread and the promise in the spiritually orphaned psalmist's cry, though I did not know the Bible: "If my father and mother forsake me, the LORD will take me up" (Ps 27:10).

My father and mother did not forsake me. Therefore, the Lord did not take me up. I know this is lousy logic and worse theology—I know it now. But during the years of my emerging young womanhood, all I felt was washed out and winded as a lone shirt pinned to a clothesline. My parents, baffled yet resolute, held one end of the line. The other end God held in a remote, unreachable hand. Thus I was not forsaken. Forsaken would have been that rotting shirt you see in the weeds by the road. I had a weathered clothespin's grasp on the sagging wire that kept me scarcely aloft in my life. Somehow I held the hell on, lest I fall down through the airy gravity that blew beneath me, a few feet above the dirty ground.

Somehow.

Somehow is a name for the saving grace of God.

The Lord is my light and my salvation; whom shall I fear?

I believe my parents meant to do well and do good in their pursuit of conventional postwar, middle-class ambitions—working at a white-collar job for him, homemaking in a nice house for her, kids for them to provide for and rear.

Why, then, this, their youngest child's chronicle of spiritual struggle?

"'Come,' my heart says, 'seek his face!' Your face, LORD, do I seek. Do not hide your face from me" (Ps 27:8-9a).

I write, like a psalmist or scribe, to pray, to seek what lies hidden, to lay down in words some years I lived through with a God wholly unbeknownst to me, whom I desired, who was as good as absent until much later. Whether outrage or the buried content of my memory's inmost pages, I write it to look for the Lord in my life and find my way to praise. This account, though personal to me, could remind you of your own history, your family, your secret hurts, and tender heart, your hunger for the holy. In other words, I was not unique and you are not alone.

Indeed, *we* are not alone. The psalmists knew this. Even the most personal and plaintive of psalmic verses—"Hear, O LORD, when I cry aloud, be gracious to me and answer me!"—is also public, liturgical, meant for the gathered worshiping people to hear and make their own (Ps 27:7). If, as some have suggested, memoir is the genre of our age, spiritual memoirs may be our books of common prayer, expressing personal lamentation and praise in terms a God-hungry communion of readers can pray.

Some writers, like some psalmists, are meant to lament, to allow readers into their tenebrous rooms. Fear not. The darkness will not overcome you. Lament long and hard enough and in the end you will find yourself nearly spent yet singing, as a woman wails through bloody childbirth to get to her lullaby, her infant. I was the last of my parents' procreative works. I love the life I'm given, shadows and all.

I look back to write forward, purposefully breaking the code of family silence so damaging to alcoholics, their spouses and children. There is a line between privacy and dishonesty, and another between revelation and exposure. I am walking these lines by writing them. I knowingly risk crossing the lines for the sake of the truth that sets people free.

My rearview gaze surveys years jabbed here and there by incidents that typify the way things were for me. Gifted with another kind of mind, one more nostalgic or optimistic, I might recall my early years more happily. What I see in hindsight is couched in family sickness, progressive and unspoken: three children coming up in a home our neighbors didn't know was broken. Daily my brother and sister and I breathed in secondhand unhappiness with the cigarette smoke that ever clouded the air around our parents. Insofar as family life broke my spirit, I felt alone. Now I know I was not unique, and in this knowledge find redemptive value that is multiplied if my story somehow edifies you. *Somehow*.

I call this a cruciform memoir. Cross-shaped. The grounded, upright beam punctures heaven. Heaven lies down luminous and broad on the earth's far horizon. Light is wrought from dark, life from death. If the girl got up—and she did, I promise you, she did get up and I am she—first she was struck down.

There it is, my theology: we are brought low and nailed down by those who either know not what they do and, meaning well, tell us it's for our own good, or just plain give us hell. We get up by the fierce mercy of One who means for us to transcend and overcome. "We" and "they" are interchangeable human parts in this theology. Sometimes we crucify the innocent; sometimes we are given up to forces the psalmist calls evildoers, adversaries, foes, and enemies.

This book is evidence of the getting up. Before I recount the resurrection, my first, necessary endeavor is to look clear back to the making of the cross and the breaking of the spirit.

Otherwise, these pages could be as rife with uncomprehending cheer as a crowded church on Easter morning. Again: don't fear. To read a cruciform memoir, even the parts about a hurting child, is to witness the testimony of the resurrected, and that can't be all bad. I write and you read in search and in the service of goodness.

Retrospection with an eye toward the eternal is the purview of both spiritual memoir and Scripture. The Bible tells its tales in the past tense to recount the history of God, to say who God was, is now, and ever shall be. So do I, with my little eye. I write in pursuit of One who deems creation good and redeems it when it goes bad. I do salvage work in search of holy love, the love that wrote the Bible: earthmoving love, medicinal love, the dying, rising love that opens graves and prayer books. I write this book because I cannot help myself. Somebody bless this mess. Bless the messengers who mean no harm but sometimes do harm anyway. Glory be to God, the giver of hazardous freedoms, forgiver of people who get things terribly wrong. God bless us, our parents and babies, our stories, our sweet and sorry lives, our psalms.

On special occasions my mother did not have to cook. My father would drive us into the city, to Greektown, where the food came pretty close to Armenian cuisine. We would walk a dark block or so from the parked car to the Parthenon Restaurant on Halsted Street. My father would bring up the rear, his hands not touching us but alert at our backs, forming an invisible shield to keep his wife and children on the sidewalk and prevent our dawdling or stepping off the curb into the gutter. A cautious man when sober, he was watchful for hazards and disinclined to pause for unplanned gawking. Once, in Greektown, as we walked past a storefront window, I was stunned by the sight of a lamb, entire and skewered, revolving over flames, juices weeping from its flesh. My mother told us that as a boy in Turkey, her father had kept a pet lamb until his parents slaughtered it for an Easter dinner he could not bring himself to eat.

Who might our parents have become if they had not become our parents? Who might my mother have become if at eighteen she had accepted the scholarship awarded her to enroll in the Sorbonne? It simply was not done. A girl, a widower's only daughter, did not take off for Paris, France, when there was a perfectly good MRS degree to pursue at a college in Texas near the home of her aunt. A hick teacher there nearly succeeded in demolishing my mother's exquisite boarding school French. So my mother transferred to a college in Wisconsin, where many of the towns bear French names.

Chicago, teeming with postwar clerical jobs for capable girls, was close by, and there were plenty of fellas to catch in the city. Back she came to Chicago and put Paris mostly out of her mind. Several years later, the suburban house where she ran in circles clothing, feeding, and cleaning up after her family bore only this reminder on a wall: a decoupage Eiffel Tower in a gilt frame, a bit of kitsch too clichéd to evoke the life my mother might have lived had she not forsaken her dreams of an international education to have a husband and children instead. Not until I, her youngest child, was fourteen did my mother seem to realize a revolution was underway, and she was invited to it.

I found half a dozen skinny cigarettes tucked in the drawer of my mother's dressing table, near her lipsticks. They were wrinkly, rolled in pink, strawberry-scented papers and enclosed in a slim plastic case that once had held a medal won at a swimming meet. Having grown a marijuana plant taller than himself in the backyard, my brother had given the joints to my mother as a parting gift before leaving home for college. So this is how it is now, I thought, and struck a match. The sweet, sharp smoke initiated me into the wonders of a drug that could make a gray day golden and turn my loneliness into a rich encounter with my thoughts.

My father intensified his nightly drinking. Though he never discussed his work with me, I suspect his employer had started making noise about "restructuring," and he was feeling insecure in his job. Alcohol in all its volatile liquidity thinned our family blood and dissolved the ties that bound us. Meanwhile, my mother strove to fashion for herself a life not circumscribed by disappointing wifedom and maddening motherhood. She took to working long hours at retail jobs in the city. She would wear back-breaking high-heeled shoes and catch the commuter train to the high-rise world of urban consumerist glamour. Underpaid but half-emancipated by day, she impressed bosses and customers with her wit and diligence.

Back at home, while my father sat stoically before the droning evening news, my mother and I engaged in screaming battles. She had discovered I had stolen not only her pot stash but also some cash from her wallet (with which I had then purchased more marijuana). I cursed and slammed, cried, and finally resorted to bleak laughter. My mother installed a lock on my parents' bedroom door and called a psychiatrist.

After I had a few forgettable appointments with this doctor, my parents admitted me to the local hospital's pediatric ward, for blood tests the purpose of which no one explained to me. Physically, I felt fine. My roommate was an eight-year-old girl in a body cast for whom I colored pictures of flowers. On the day I expected to go home, a nurse told me, "You have one more test. But you can get into your street clothes." I put on a velour pullover my mother had sewn for me and was made to ride in a wheelchair. The elevator jostled to a stop and its doors opened to a placard that read, "Psychiatric Locked Unit 2 North."

My new hospital roommate was a tiny old woman named Josephine. I once returned from the shower room to find that despite her obvious frailty, Josephine had managed to pull my steel-framed bed away from the wall. She was crouching behind it. When I asked her what she was doing, she hissed at me, "They're coming!" Later an orderly told me, "Josephine spent some time in a concentration camp. So, you know, she's a little delusional. Just go along with what she says."

I spent my first few days in 2 North weeping into the pay phone in the hall, begging my mother to let me come home, promising to be good from now on. She did not relent. I ultimately did relent and settled into life on the ward.

I now think of my seven inpatient weeks as my first brush with monasticism. Of course I lacked the terminology to say so at the time, but there was something of a liturgy of hours, a rhythm of *ora et labora* (prayer and work) in the calm and ordered hospital days. At 7:30, you ate breakfast with others. At 10:30, you went to Group Therapy. At 3:00, you made crafts. And there was a community—of crazies, naturally— but they welcomed me, told me how grownup I seemed for a girl of only fourteen and how good it was that the shrink was not doping me with psychotropic drugs.

One patient, pretty and thirtyish, sometimes spoke wistfully of her suicide attempts. She told me, "Honey, you seem just fine. I want my son to meet you." The ward provided me with a patterned respite from the half-speechless, half-cacophonous climate of home. Nurses and patients alike told me they admired the fact that I would sit at a table in the patients' common room, ignoring the TV, writing in a diary.

I felt virtuous and hopeful when reading or writing. I read *The Great Gatsby*. Gatsby is hardly a character to emulate, but this fact escaped me as I went with my impulse, prompted by a scene near the novel's end. After Gatsby's lonesome, gangsterish death, his hayseed father, Mr. Gatz, proudly shows Nick Carraway the self-improvement schedule Gatsby composed in a diary as young man.

"Find a religion," I wrote in my own diary.

Religion had something to do with goodness and purity. The hospital had been founded by Seventh Day Adventists.

I detected little of their influence except at meals, which were meatless and devoid of such stimulants as pepper and caffeine. If I could find a faith, it would need to be something transcendent, strong enough to lift me up and out of the pain of daily life and infuse my being with serenity, order, gladness, dignity, and purpose. I thought about these things as I tidied my hospital room, smoothing and tucking in the bedsheets. My little radio played rock music, sometimes of a new sort, jangling and spare. "Take me to the water," a man yelped in a song. He sounded both inspired and possessed, barking and hooting about the river he had in mind.

I will never know what the psychiatrist had in mind for my seven-week hospital stay. I do know it allowed my parents unwittingly to scapegoat their problem child and incarcerate me, telling me and themselves everything was for my own good. They did—let's face it—what some parents only dream of doing with their incorrigible adolescent kids. My mother's own parents had sent her to boarding school at age fourteen, to "protect" her from witnessing her mother's grueling struggle with colon cancer. My mother repeated the banishment she knew, while my father evidently assented, "Whatever you say."

To my knowledge, the psychiatrist was unaware of the alcoholism and attendant psychological afflictions in our family. By now both my siblings had gone away to college. The doctor did not treat the family. He treated me—to periodic visits with him, unsmiling in his boxy leather chair, a substantial gold chain adorning his wrist. He came across as smug and disapproving, as though he had uncritically bought the line that I was a bad girl, out of control. If ever he wondered why I had become unmanageable, he never traced the cause back to the family dynamic. He was in the business of locking up unruly women. During my inpatient stint, he admitted his own sister to the ward. This caused quite a hubbub among the patients, many of whom trash-talked him during Free Time, when we crammed into the smoking lounge and sucked on cigarettes. Have I mentioned that most of the patients were women?

More often than I met with the psychiatrist, I met with the psychiatric social worker, a ginger-haired man with a withered arm and a folksy yet provocative manner. I once overheard him concluding a phone conversation with the words, "We'll wine her and dine her, dice her and slice her."

He hung up and welcomed me to take a seat for our scheduled appointment in his office. "That was my business partner," he explained. "We're meeting with an investor. We invented a gas-saving thing for cars, and we're gonna make a million bucks."

"Wow."

"Hey, I heard you listening to Janis Joplin in your room."

"Yeah."

"Only white woman who could ever sing the blues. You got the blues?"

"I'm alright."

"You masturbate?"

"What? No."

"Come on. You can admit it. You masturbate, right?"

"I said no."

"You sure?"

I wanted to be good—not as good, perhaps, as the candy stripers I recognized from high school, girls I sometimes saw whispering and glancing my way in the hospital's halls, but not as bad as those girls likely thought I was. How emboldening it would have been to stumble on the book of Psalms back then. All that seething, soaring poetry, those swings from paranoia to adoration, might have helped my heart take courage while I waited for the Lord. Secretly I still hoped God was waiting for me in the land of the living, if only I could find my way there.

The day I was released from the psychiatric ward, my mother informed she would be taking me to Europe at the end of the week. She had visited Rome the summer before and had met a Lebanese hotelier who now put us both up—I in my own room some distance down the hall from my mother's. At fourteen, I was blond and green-eyed, cute and nubile. Men on the Roman streets leered and stalked, idiotic predators. I felt hunted and endangered but also thrilled and curious.

We remained in Rome for three full weeks, my mother leaving me alone for stretches of hours in the afternoons. I consorted with street vendors—not a savory bunch—on the Spanish Steps. I wound up all over the eternal city—behind a fallen pillar in the Roman Forum, in an hourly rated *pensione*, in the backseat of a Fiat, at a makeshift photography studio. I was readily taken up and just as swiftly cast off by Massimo, Biagio, Lauro, Vincenzo, and a soldier whose name I forget, who taught me the Italian slang for fellatio, which I remember.

In the shadows of spectacular but empty Roman churches, I learned to be desirable to men. In the Vatican I learned the church was a museum. Outside its grand and guarded doors, grubby children pawed the tourists, begging for a few hundred *lire*. The world was surely godless, and the religion of Rome a gorgeous distraction from the fact. But under the heavenless sky, there were glorious earthly pleasures to enjoy: the creamy, piquant noodles at a restaurant called Alfredo's, the astonishingly potent, sweet flavors packed into a paper cup of gelato.

There was wine, too, glass after glass of wine, and aged stone stairwells to stagger down bellowing, drunk with my latest Roman boyfriend. In piazza fountains, marble gods lounged day and night, naked except for a layer of exhaust grime. I splashed my face with cool city water, as if that would sober me up. It would not, and neither would a doll-sized cup of espresso, bitter, sugary, and hot. Aquiline-nosed friars in long black dresses hurried up and down the sidewalk-width streets, too intent on holy business to bestow a passing blessing on a hapless American girl. Drivers parked their demitasse-sized cars in flowerpots. All the shameless Romans' laundered underwear flew, baggy little flags pinned to strings outside their windows.

Once the fun and money ran out, my mother and I flew home wearing brand new leather shoes, bearing heartaches we kept from each other. I could see hers in her eyes. She was forty-four years old, returning from a foreign escapade to the dull facts of her life. I was fourteen years old, the age she had been when her mother finished sewing a dress for her, lay down on the davenport, and died. The unhappiness of her fourteen-year-old daughter seems to have been unbearable for her to reckon with at forty-four. Hence her decisions to lock me away, then haul me overseas to leave me in the care of strangers while she did what Romans do.

Would it be in better taste to keep this story to myself? It's less good taste I'm after than to taste and see that God is good—God, whom a psalmist claims is "near to the brokenhearted, and saves the crushed in spirit" (Ps 34:18). At fourteen, I was both brokenhearted and crushed. I can scarcely imagine how deeply broken was my mother's own heart, how completely crushed her spirit, when at fourteen she lost her mother to cancer. Three decades on, perhaps the outraged psyche of the middle-aged woman reverberated with the shock of mother-death. Motherless, lacking any memory of a model she could follow, she could not properly mother the daughter who perhaps reminded her of her young abandoned self. To hell with you, she told her child in effect, having learned adulthood—or at least its chronological semblance—must be entered alone by way of heartbreak.

Having seen some of Italy's staggering sacred art, I now found the suburbs terribly banal. I would sometimes put on a skirt and walk with a slender book in hand to the little business district of our town. There I hoped to meet someone who would understand how it was with me, how my young soul knew ageless pain and beauty. I was sitting in a coffee shop eating a salad, reading about Michelangelo, when a man somewhere in his fifties slid into the seat opposite mine in the booth. How intelligent I must have been, he said, to be reading such a book.

He introduced himself as Phil and said he was the restaurant's proprietor. Within minutes he had offered me the worst sort of job, scraping grease from the grill at the end of each workday, wiping down the spattered kitchen surfaces. Underage as I was, this was work I could do for a few tax-free dollars at a rate beneath minimum wage. My presence in the restaurant gave Phil the opportunity to talk art with me and joke around, pointing to the protrusion in his trousers. "It happens," he once told me, "when I watch you clean."

A restaurant regular, a woman who said she was divorced and sold steel for a living, would stop in for a glass of iced tea after the commuter train returned her, weary, to the suburbs. She once summoned me to her side at the counter while Phil was busy serving other customers.

"Have you heard of Mount Holyoke?" she whispered.

I looked at her.

"It's a girl's school. Phil was a professor there. Tenured. Do you know what tenure is?"

I shook my head.

"Let's just say it's not easy to fire a tenured professor, but they finally fired Phil. What I'm saying is, Rachel, you're too bright for this job."

"The Lord is near to the brokenhearted, and saves the crushed in spirit" (Ps 34:18). The first time I read the psalm that makes this claim, I knew it to be true: there is a correlation between suffering and the sacred. Loss or deprivation, abuse or exploitation grind the human spirit. Like the scent of pulverized spices, then, prayers rise up to the Lord, who is at hand, sometimes in the form of a stranger.

American boys, I found, were not as frank or interesting as Romans. Musky and lean, by turns urgent and avoidant, American boys wanted cars, beer, weed, sex, and a whole a lot of Led Zeppelin. Two or more of these combined in an evening could hazily substitute for love. Love, wailed the radio songs, could make me happy way down inside. But I never got love, I never got happy, and I never met a boy who wanted the abiding love of one girl. I met boys who sometimes wanted a girl at loose ends whose parents paid little mind to what time she came home and in what shape. Self-disregard came easily to me and made me as easy to take as to leave.

Between the taking and the leaving, when I was wanted, I existed. In this interval I sometimes heard my name, its two lambish syllables devotional and hushed. My name voiced by a boy confirmed I mattered momentarily. To receive a boy's attention—the fleeting gift of his regard, however groping its expression—became my guiding purpose, my pursuit of happiness.

Before the sexed-up 1970s ended, I returned to high school with rolling papers in my purse. My unchanged home life, removed from the hospital's clinical disciplines and *bella Roma*'s decadence, worsened my sense of suburban captivity and deepened my desire to smoke my way to oblivion.

I tried halfheartedly to reform myself, attending a couple of chaperoned outings with friends who belonged to a synagogue's and a church's youth groups. These trips, to an amusement park and to the movies, respectively, struck me as weirdly irreligious. But what did I know? I rode the Tilt-a-Whirl and watched *Coming Home* with the other fifteen-year-olds, secretly hoping that somehow these activities would lead me toward a god who could help me. When I stepped out of the movie theater, I heard my mother call my name in a familiar *gotcha* tone. I saw her car parked across the street, her displeased face watching me through the open driver's side window. Clearly I was no better a girl than before, and now I was busted again.

The guidance counselor at the high school, a freckled, benevolent whale of a woman, recommended an alternative school for troubled kids. My parents, who had been known in the past to take an expert's advice on how to handle me, removed me from the public high school. They sent me to learn at the feet of a few well-meaning souls who rented the second floor in a decrepit former elementary school. I carpooled there and back with three neighboring boys, one of whom drove a bronze-colored Chevy Chevette. Along with the handful of other last-chance stoners who comprised the alternative school's student body, I called my new teachers by their first names and took courses in The Sixties, Hypnosis, Women's Literature, and Ethics.

Oh, Jim, the Ethics teacher, with his pale blue eyes and his big Christian heart. Teaching Ethics was his part-time job, which he did when not attending classes to become a minister. A minister, I gradually learned, is what every one of my new teachers was or would soon be. Chuck, Beatrice, Norm, Barbara, Jim—each of them, it turned out, believed in God and Jesus in a big way. Barbara had a picture of Jesus, looking sandy-haired and kind, in her wallet. Our teachers did not teach religion classes, but we were free to "rap" with them about questions of faith if we chose. Chuck, the school's lead teacher, once took me out to lunch at a restaurant where the sandwiches were garnished with sprouts and served on hand-thrown pottery plates. Copies of a paperback book called *Desire of Ages* were on offer in a basket, free of charge. Chuck was so mellow and earthy with his beard and his vintage Jeep, he made religion seem cool.

But religion, I had decided in Rome, was a muraled monument to an illusion. Or, as I had determined on returning to the States, it was an entertainment that no more pointed to God than a frescoed cathedral did. I was quick to form opinions based on scraps of information and flashes of feeling. When I looked back on Our Father's apparent refusal to answer my childhood prayers, and combined that disappointment with my teenage first impressions of Jewish and Christian religion, I came up with nothing, which is what I then resented God for being. I ruefully concurred with Patti Smith's punk heresy: "Jesus died for somebody's sins, but not mine."

I had no God to sin against. This was not a comfort. When there is no deity to offend, neither is there one who will forgive. An atheist's life is bleaker than a sinner's if deep down the atheist wishes God were there. Life was bleak not because my parents sinned against me with malice of forethought or contempt, but because in our family, we each lacked (or believed we lacked) anyone to turn to but ourselves. In our separate narcissisms, we turned against each other.

Miraculously, while our family disintegrated, my alternative schoolteachers, Chuck and Beatrice, took interest in me. They praised my writing and encouraged me to enter a local essay contest, which I won. The newspaper published not my essay but a photograph of me shaking hands with the banker whose savings and loan had donated the hundred-dollar cash prize I won. Had it been published, my essay, a morose but skillfully composed meditation on vacuous public education, might have caused ill will among members of the local public school board. All I knew was that I now wanted to make a bold mark, speak my hurting but creative mind, and do something more productive than sink into a stoned fog.

Marijuana had lost its appeal, having devolved from a reality-enhancer to a thought-warping, limb-numbing time-waster. This was progress. I sensed a new day at hand and wanted to put it into words. My parents, largely indifferent to my interests, went about pursuing their own. A handful of other adults, religious Christians who bothered teaching kids on the verge of dropping out, believed I had something worthy to say. They were just as encouraging of my dispirited, underachieving classmates. Our teachers addressed us as grownups, referring to the girls as "women" and the boys as "men."

I would force myself to look away from Jim the Ethics teacher's blue eyes and think about the right thing to do. I decided to speak up for safety. I told Chuck that the three "men" with whom I carpooled to and from school commonly passed around a fifth of Jack Daniel's during the drive. Unlike my former associates in the psych ward, I had no interest in dying a tragic and untimely death.

Somehow I had become a girl with a sense of self-preservation and nerve enough to narc on her reckless peers.

Soon after I confided in Chuck about the whiskeyed commutes in the flimsy bronze Chevette, the demeanor of the three other carpoolers sobered markedly. For a while, these guys had liked me. Now I liked myself well enough to withstand their disdain. During the drives to school and back, they blatantly left me out of conversations and ignored me when I spoke. I folded my arms, glared at the scenery, and thought, *Be that way. See if I care.* This I could handle. This was nothing. I had been dealing with God's silent treatment for years.

CHAPTER

3

Her Ways Wander

In springtime, as new grasses emerge in bright, silky blades, Chicagoans young and old come out to play in city parks and on lakefront beaches. People haul out their sun-hungry bodies and run, bike, and picnic by the lake. They revel in weather sweetened at last by fresh rays hot enough to melt the sky's white parka and reveal its blue, true self. The season of festivals and fireworks begins, the season of glare and softened road tar, of naked limbs and near-naked hearts.

Not because of brilliance on my part, but because (despite all the sincerity of its teachers) the alternative high school lacked state accreditation and its standards were iffy, I graduated at age sixteen. As soon as I had obtained my dubious diploma, at every opportunity friends and I would catch the Burlington Northern train out of the suburbs into the city. Chicago's big mirror of a lake lined by equally mirrored towers drew us out of our placid homogeneous community. On boulevards downtown we caught roaring, hissing busses, feeling grownup and risqué and free among the seasoned riders.

One day my friend Jill and I packed strawberries and cheeses in a basket and set out for what we imagined would be a rather European urban picnic. Like me, she had attended the alternative high school and had graduated early, under-prepared for adulthood. Look out, world, here we came in our sundresses. Saturday, warm and full of possibility, spread out before us like a blanket on the grass.

At the time of this writing, I could be the middle-aged mother of those two adventuring girls. I could envy their slender, firm flesh, and I could certainly fear for their lives. Or—imagine this—I could chaperone them and mandate a curfew. As it was, Jill's mother had undergone so many electroshock therapy treatments that just getting out of bed was a task. When she managed it, she watched TV in a house frock, tears rolling down her plump, expressionless face. Jill's absent father supported himself selling dope and collecting disability benefits somewhere in Michigan. Jill rarely saw him, and I never met him. Our parents, Jill's and my own, each found ways not to know what their teenaged daughters were up to. Thus no one could object when I smiled for the camera pointed at me by a mustachioed man in a city park one sunny Saturday.

I knew how to do this. I had been to Rome and back, and I knew how to vamp just enough to hold a man's gaze. It was easy with this man. He was in the gazing business. Behind the camera and its forthright cylindrical lens, his face was not handsome. But it was more his looking than his looks that interested me. I made small, instinctual adjustments, lowering my chin a fraction, lifting my eyes to the camera's black orifice. Muscles tugged at the corners of my mouth to make my face happy for a stranger stranger than most.

It's not every day you meet an Amish photographer.

To be accurate, Gideon was not Amish any longer. A decade or so earlier, his bishop in rural Illinois had excommunicated him for sneaking off to a Mennonite college. Had Gideon thought the leader of his separatist sect would overlook such a transgression? The Amish, exempt from compulsory education laws, keep their young people out of "English" (non-Amish) high schools in order to protect the purity of their community. College is out of the question. Gideon had not deliberately set out to quit his faith or his people. But in the late 1960s, one thing led him to another. Conscientious objection to military service led him, in lieu of the draft and Vietnam, to a menial job in a hospital staffed by comparatively worldly men and women. From there he ventured to Indiana, where he paid his tuition with funds from his prosperous farming family, until they cut him off and cut him loose at the urging of the bishop.

Gideon picked up a camera and literally wandered the world after that, taking up temporarily in New Orleans, Mexico City, Paris, New York, and now, Chicago. Members of his community of origin, true to their rigorous Bible-based customs, formally shunned him for refusing to belong to them body and soul. Now he did not belong to anyone anywhere.

As peculiar a species as is an Amish photographer, Gideon made ironic sense. Bred by religious people so iconoclastic their children's baby dolls bore blank socks for faces, he renounced the Amish way by aggressively pursuing what the Amish deemed idolatrous and sinful: picture-taking, not to mention higher education and fornication. Moreover, he wore a moustache, not a beard without one, and drove a Fiat Spider, not a horse and buggy.

Soon after Gideon took my picture, we became a couple. He was thirty-two years old, twice my age and lacking any qualms of which I was aware to committing the statutory rape of a minor. Given his origins among a people who defied most mainstream American mores, I doubt a sixteen-year-old female seemed to him too young a partner for a grown man. In all probability, Gideon's sisters had married at roughly that age.

The first time I phoned my mother to tell her I would not be coming home from Gideon's, she sounded bemused, vaguely proud. She did not consult my father while we were on the telephone. Though my liaison with this older man seemed to give my father pause throughout its eighteen-month duration, he never openly objected to the arrangement. The problems (parents relinquishing their teenage daughter to a man in his thirties, the same man sexually exploiting a girl who could not comprehend her situation as abusive) are plain to me now. Back then, however, I considered myself an unimpeded woman, precocious and ready to make my own choices.

Only in physique was I a woman. Otherwise, I remained a girl possessed of an absorbent but largely undisciplined intellect, emotional impulsiveness, high verbal abilities, and a soul that briefly, years earlier, had glimpsed the presence of the holy in the kitchen. I saw the world as in a scratched and dirty mirror. Surrounding my marred reflection were the slightly warped, evolving faces of those who came and went in my life but never clarified it: parents, doctors, counselors, teachers, lovers.

Gideon and I enjoyed the simpatico of two exiles each granted a breather from loneliness. Unmoored, a vagabond greedily observant of others' appearances, he employed his camera like a spyglass. He rarely related with the people he photographed, but documented them to watch them later on, emerging on paper, shadowy and colorless, anonymous in their developing baths. Unlike Amish dolls, the subjects of Gideon's pictures had faces. He was not one to wonder much about the mind behind a face, or, for that matter, about the character inside a woman's flesh (or a girl's). I sometimes assisted him in his makeshift darkroom. We also slept in there on a foam mattress surrounded by piles of black and white prints. They revealed his voyeuristic gift for capturing in public (where he was always watching) couples canoodling and young women flattered by his frank attentions.

Contrary to his lusty rootlessness, Gideon would sing hymns to Jesus while washing up his few mismatched cups and plates. For more than twenty years, hymns a capella had been the only music in Gideon's ears. And what music: he and his multiple siblings had sung hymns in four-part harmony over the intercom system some doctrinal loophole had allowed his parents to install in their farmhouse. Gideon's now solo tenor vocal made the name of Jesus sound both glorious and familiar. When I heard it, something flared inside me—jealousy of someone so beloved his name alone comprised a lyric and a melody, and envy of Gideon's spiritual access to this man whose religion he no longer practiced, yet whose mere name could still inspire him to sing.

Hymns tethered Gideon to the tradition from which he rambled far but did not entirely reject. His parents, his neighbors, worship and manual work, Midwestern farmland, the guttural Pennsylvania Dutch dialect, Scripture and song, his siblings in their drab and buttonless attire—all of these seemed to represent in Gideon's memory a sensible system for inhabiting the planet decently with others. Hymns reconnected him to an ordered way of life and the Savior at its center. They lent Gideon a sense of meaning and an interior compass to which he still could refer, if only to mark his point of departure.

If remembered, outgrown religion is what I heard in Gideon's hymns, it is also what I see in my father's First Communion portrait. The photo of a solemn boy in knee-length trousers, holding a rosary, is one of my bittersweet treasures. What became of that little catechumen in the picture? Fortified by lard-and-onion sandwiches on rye bread, he could jitterbug with the best of them. Later, like the rest of them, he enlisted in the army, replacing the crucifix with a dog tag. Any mysticism that may have infused his early Roman Catholic formation seems not to have deeply impressed his naturally analytical and skeptical mind, though he did retain an anxious sense of right and wrong. A person should do the right thing and fear the consequence of the alternative. The church, the neighborhood nuns, and parish priests had taught him to be dutiful and judicious. That he was, though by no means religious in my lifetime.

My father seemed content at times. I remember him intently watching the Chicago Blackhawks on TV, shouting, "Hey, hey!" when the puck flew past the other team's goalie. "Hey, hey!" overheard bespoke manly spontaneous gladness. Dadness, you could call it, had it carried over to the rest of us. It rarely did. There was a complex, interesting man inside that lanky Lithuanian figure, but I never got to know him well. He kept such a close watch on himself I am hard-pressed to tell you what he gave me beyond a Baltic genealogy that may explain why my eyes are green and my shoulders fairly broad. I suppose I also inherited some of my writing ability from him. My father did not and could not teach me faith. Through that omission and other commissions, with my mother he raised up the girl who came to be so lonely for God I did whatever I could to be beheld appreciatively, even, if need be, by a low-grade pedophile with a camera.

I matured into the woman writing this book. I write with respect for honesty that compels me to address topics on which I might be silent if decorum were my aim. Faithfulness is my aim; God is my aim. I mean to look within the actions of my story's characters for signs of the God I long missed. This book is a labor of redemptive retrieval I know no other way to undertake. I find myself as determined to write it as Gideon was to sing his hymns. We cannot shake our memories, but we can repurpose them as truthful if quite subjective stories, as work songs or proverbs, lessons learned by accident or taught to us by dedicated teachers.

The narrator of the book of Proverbs recalls a dedicated teacher: "When I was a son with my father, tender, and my mother's favorite, he taught me, and said to me, 'Let your heart hold fast my words; keep my commandments, and live. Get wisdom; get insight; do not forget, nor turn away from the words of my mouth'" (4:3-5).

If the teachings are not dogma-choked, if God is glorified and the religion itself is not deified, then religious formation in a caring faith community seems to me a very fine gift for parents to give a child. When I was a daughter, words of wisdom and insight were not what my father was able to give me, even though I could tell he had a sharp mind. I yearned for him to impart something to me I could grow on. As for my mother, I am sure she felt her love for me powerfully. I experienced it as a hunger I was expected to feed as though doing so was my reason for being, which I knew instinctively it was not. When it came to love, my responsibility as a kid was on one hand to do without and make do, and on the other hand to perform and gratify. What I wanted was some version of the abundant, unqualified, instructive, sometimes chastening parental love portrayed in the book of Proverbs.

Proverbs consists largely of a father's moral teachings for his son, in antiquity. Proverbs cannot re-parent me or easily infuse me with the wisdom and insight the book is meant to impart. Ancient and deeply patriarchal though it is, Proverbs nevertheless turns out to be a worthy source to inform a contemporary woman's cruciform memoir. The crux of the cruciform is, after all, the intersection of divergent directions, where opposites meet, not resolving but confronting one another to reveal something true, as paradoxes do. So I look for God in a past from which God seemed absent. I retrace my religious formation in an upbringing devoid of sacred teaching. I look for wisdom and insight in a man's old book inherently hostile to a woman like me, who is critical of female caricatures such as those in Proverbs.

I glimpse myself, cruciform, paradoxical, and whole, in Proverbs' two female figures—the woman of wisdom and the dangerous stranger. The biblical author intends for his readers to choose one woman over the other: wisdom over folly; "the wife of your youth" (5:18) over the adulteress; the "intimate friend" over the prostitute (7:4). Proverbs' moral world, personified in these feminine symbols, is dichotomous, like my father's sense of right and wrong. In the proverbial world reside the good girl or wise woman, and the bad girl or wicked woman. I am neither wicked nor wise. I'm a little of both and then some, so I identify with both, rejecting neither. When I was younger, I tried to choose up sides, to be only bad or good. Either way, I denied and amputated something vital of myself until, well into womanhood, I began to claim the whole dichotomy as me, and not just one half or the other.

My family of origin and my own young spirit were fractured in part by our untenable conviction that we could and should be and feel only good. Disallowed and banished from awareness was anything truly bad, whether it was my mother's ancestral memory of genocide, her bitter adolescent grief at the death of her mother, the impact on my father of his impoverished childhood, the killing he knew as a soldier, or the impact of his alcoholism on us all.

No one taught my parents to lament their losses. Lamentation is a practice that can lead the liberating way to hope and gratitude. Without releasing grief, the living stay stuck in their catastrophes and tend to visit them upon their children. Proverbs can be misused to promote a simplistic morality in which some people are deemed "bad." My mother and father were not bad, but young once, and vulnerable. And this world, to which God grants great freedom, aggrieved and infuriated them. Later, they did their postwar best to stay this side of hell, to marry well, feel fine, and raise good kids. Their sadness had no open outlet. Nor did regret, nor anger, nor any individual variation from the master plan for familial happiness our family strove to fulfill by sheer will. Perhaps our most painful mistake was to try to live as though mistakes and pain could be avoided. We would have been better off with a more complex and integrated outlook, allowing room for sorrow and fury, for neutrality, uncertainty, and genuine, not fabricated, happiness.

As a kid I knew there was more to reality than my mother and father permitted themselves or their children to experience. At a primal level, we three kids understood hostility, aggression, anxiety, heartache, and lust needed somewhere to go. If we had been allowed to express these within sane boundaries, then beauty and gentleness, serenity, affection, and passion would also have found their rightful expression in our family. But control was the idol of my parents—self-control through the anesthetizing sacrament of alcohol, and control of others through self-indulgent tyranny.

As systemically sick families commonly do, ours chose a scapegoat—me—on whose back to heap the shame of disowned urges and emotions. Unpleasant feelings would have exposed our family's ambivalent humanity, which is a messier, more complicated condition than simply being good, right and happy. Ambivalence, the layered, unpredictable blend of good and bad, of right and wrong and other, subtler responses, is a more honest way of being than we dared.

We lived in fear of pain, far from God, in whose rich image we were made but didn't know it. As the family scapegoat, I often lived in fear *and* pain, with the strong sense that God was far from me. I was the bad girl, the loose woman whom the book of Proverbs warns against. Her seductive allure is resistible only by the forceful application of wisdom, which begins in the good old fear of the Lord: "If you indeed cry out for insight, and raise your voice for understanding; if you seek it like silver, and search for it as for hidden treasures—

then you will understand the fear of the LORD and find the knowledge of God" (2:3-5).

Gideon, raised to be a God-fearing man in a strict and narrow sense, transgressed the confinements of Amish biblical ethics by pursuing the proverbial bad girl whose role I played not only in behavior but also in my teenaged lack of self-awareness: "She does not keep straight to the path of life; her ways wander, and she does not know it" (Prov 5:6).

The work of redemptive retrieval at the heart of this cruciform memoir obliges me to search for wisdom in the very sources of my wounding. I would like the whole story to be happier. I want, as much as my parents wanted, for life not to hurt. But God showed up unbidden in the middle of the pain. In the kitchen, the customary domain of womanhood where my mother subsumed her identity in domestic drudgery, alone and small I sensed the holy living presence. It offered me the possibility of a spiritually larger life than the one I saw my parents living, but only on the condition that I grow up to sacrifice certain comforts and illusions for the sake of honesty.

This book is sacrificial in the sense that I am giving up any pretense that I came to faith by way of wisdom parentally imparted in affection and good health. Why would such a pretense even occur to me to promote? I am a church lady and a professional one at that. I'm a pastor and a preacher in a mainline Protestant tradition, where middle-class expectations of normalcy and propriety continue to hold sway. Clergy are still preferably male, cradle Christian, heterosexual, and married with children whom their wives are raising to be good boys and girls who love Jesus, just as mom and dad were raised. I have the heterosexuality and marriage covered. But as a childless female adult convert to Christianity with mystical leanings and several progressive theological ideas, I transgress some boundaries of normalcy, departing too far from it for some churchgoers' comfort. They occasionally

leave the church I serve for congregations whose pastors'
chromosomal makeup and orthodoxy reassure. I can't com-
pete with those guys, and I don't try to. I do something else
clergy are expected not to do: I write and publish stories
about myself in which sex, drugs, and family secrets figure.
It's unseemly. I hereby sacrifice any image of seemliness I
might once have wished to project.

There are far tougher sacrifices to make than publicly
admitting you're a spiritually searching woman with a dys-
functional family and some youthful misadventures in your
past. If this memoir is truly to be cruciform, I must sacrifice
the fantasy popular among Christians that the new life in
Christ may be attained without suffering and death. The
cross emptied of Jesus' tortured corpse is the preferred Protestant symbol. Beautiful though the empty cross can be, it
also bespeaks a queasiness concerning the human hardships
and horrors from which we need salvation.

Hidden in the suffering and death, the promise of new
life lies buried. Resurrection reaps the new life crucifixion
sowed. Any wisdom or knowledge in this book is a fruit that
grew on the family tree from whose boughs a cross was also
hewn. Who could blame my parents for abstaining from the
religion of the cross? It involves a ghastly premise. Suffering-
avoidant alternatives abound.

Suffering-avoidance was the name of my family's game,
and that made us no different from much of the general
population. But once I underwent the kitchen revelation,
I was different. I was given awareness of movements and
meanings beneath the surfaces of situations. It was the kind
of consciousness my parents ignored and even ridiculed by
rejecting all things religious. It was forbidden, a secret life
I had to keep concealed. Yet this inner life of mine consisted partly of a contemplative appetite that—what do you
know?—resembled my father's quiet temperament, and
partly of a capacity for passion comparable to my mother's.

Even in differentiating myself from them, I remained my father's and my mother's daughter. My wholeness in adulthood obliges me to acknowledge—and gratefully too—that despite all my young rebellions and departures, I learned a thing or two from my parents.

I am tempted to bifurcate my story into false halves: bad and good, lost and found, crucified and risen. According to these dualities, I now occupy the better half of my life—a tidy thought given that, chronologically speaking at the time of this writing, I was baptized half my life ago. But two-sided thinking would do injustice to the God whose way is to transgress imagined barriers that separate the profane from the sacred. If I take seriously the Christian doctrine of the Trinity (and I do), then I must admit that the eternal God appears uninvited in the world and was as much present and at work in my life before my baptism as in the sacrament itself and afterward. God was and is never absent, never barred, only unacknowledged.

Immanuel after all. God is with us. God was with my family in ways I cannot tell to this day. Though I may seem at times to suggest that God was actually banished from our lives, I know that to argue such a claim would be absurd. How dare I say where God was not? All I can reasonably hope to say is what I experienced and how I think about it now in light of any faithful wisdom I have gained.

The book of Proverbs talks in if-then terms about rewards, chiefly wisdom, that we reap through our best efforts. It is not a book big on grace, the undeserved and unearned gifts of God that befall the bad and good girl, the listless and the diligent alike. A compendium of religious logic, Proverbs portrays the Lord as doling out consequences in response to human choices. This suggests that in the final analysis, it is I, not God, who am responsible for wising me up: "If you indeed cry out for insight, and raise your voice for understanding;

if you seek it like silver, and search for it as for hidden treasures—then you will understand the fear of the LORD and find the knowledge of God" (Prov 2:3-5).

In contrast to Proverbs' bad girl (the streetwalking seductress who leads impressionable young men to their ruin), Wisdom, personified as a virtuous female, lifts her voice in the public square. She announces the doom and diagnosis of the foolish: "Those who miss me injure themselves; all who hate me love death" (Prov 8:36). Wisdom makes this declaration with no mercy for those who miss her. We get what we deserve according to the moral code of Proverbs. To extrapolate accordingly, I deservedly suffered as a foolish young woman for deploying all the charms I could to attain love or its facsimile.

Something's wrong with this justice system. Cherry-picking Scripture doesn't fix it. Biblical interpreters who locate sacred Sophia (the Greek name for Wisdom) in Proverbs and uphold her as a paragon of divine female empowerment tend to overlook a lot: Wisdom is merciless toward the foolish; Wisdom's renown is problematically contrasted with the depravity of Proverbs' despised "loose woman"; men composed the book of Proverbs for men in a conceptual scheme that treated women as stereotyped literary devices, not as human beings with our own moral agency and religious interests.

For a woman to identify with biblical Wisdom and see in herself a manifestation of scriptural Sophia is implicitly to reject female experience that does not conform to the sexual and moral standards of Near Eastern patriarchy in antiquity. Such selective use of Scripture keeps the good stuff and ignores the ugly and oppressive stuff. I reject Sophia spirituality that disowns the aspects of female life Proverbs deems wicked. I prefer to reclaim Proverb's wicked woman, to announce that she is in me and that in Christ I am no longer ashamed of myself, even for damaging choices I once made that would scandalize the instructive father-narrator of Proverbs. His book, by no means irredeemable, is a tool. Its limitations don't limit my search for holy wisdom but encourage it, if mainly by way of irritation.

"Wisdom is vindicated by all her children," says Jesus (Luke 7:35). From this bold word, which he speaks to moralizing critics who disparaged both John the Baptist and the Son of Man, I take comfort and courage to press on. I honor the child I was, in whom holy fear and wisdom flickered in the kitchen, in the playroom, under bedcovers as I prayed a clandestine prayer. The flicker flamed out and a long darkness took over. Wounded and confused for years, I injured God's beloved child, myself. I undoubtedly confounded others as well. I believe I remained beloved of God all that time. I believe all children, including the fifth wheel, the mouthy little scapegoat, the thief, the slut, the stoner, the girl who's so much trouble they say she has to be locked up—all children vindicate the wisdom of God, who loves foolishly enough to have loved me when I could have been written off.

Why do I believe? On what basis do I claim God loves the likes of me, and profligately too? In a word: Jesus. Just two verses after Luke has Jesus pronouncing wisdom's vindication by her children, a woman shows up uninvited (the way God tends to show up in the world). The woman bears a striking resemblance to Wisdom's loose and sinful counterpart in the book of Proverbs. Yet with hospitality, gratitude, generosity, and in stark contradiction to the exclusionary mores of his culture and his dinner host, Jesus loves her. As have many other women, I am sure, I take this story personally.

> One of the Pharisees asked Jesus to eat with him, and he went into the Pharisee's house and took his place at the table. And a woman in the city, who was a sinner, having learned that he was eating in the Pharisee's house, brought an alabaster jar of ointment. She stood behind him at his feet, weeping, and began to bathe his feet with her tears and

to dry them with her hair. Then she continued kissing his feet and anointing them with the ointment. Now when the Pharisee who had invited him saw it, he said to himself, "If this man were a prophet, he would have known who and what kind of woman this is who is touching him—that she is a sinner." Jesus spoke up and said to him, "Simon, I have something to say to you." "Teacher," he replied, "Speak." "A certain creditor had two debtors; one owed five hundred denarii, and the other fifty. When they could not pay, he canceled the debts for both of them. Now which of them will love him more?" Simon answered, "I suppose the one for whom he canceled the greater debt." And Jesus said to him, "You have judged rightly." Then turning toward the woman, he said to Simon, "Do you see this woman? I entered your house; you gave me no water for my feet, but she has bathed my feet with her tears and dried them with her hair. You gave me no kiss, but from the time I came in she has not stopped kissing my feet. You did not anoint my head with oil, but she has anointed my feet with ointment. Therefore, I tell you, her sins, which were many, have been forgiven; hence she has shown great love. But the one to whom little is forgiven, loves little." Then he said to her, "Your sins are forgiven." But those who were at the table with him began to say among themselves, "Who is this who even forgives sins?" And he said to the woman, "Your faith has saved you; go in peace." (Luke 7:36-50)

Incarnated in the city woman I see full female humanity, the convergence of savvy, chutzpah, recklessness, humiliation, sorrow, sensuality, contrition, resourcefulness, kindness, piety, and freedom. God knows—we don't—the nature of her personal past, which led Luke and the Pharisee he portrays to call her a sinner. It's commonly assumed her sins were sexual, that she was a prostitute, and she was Mary Magdalene. These assumptions can reduce the city woman to a type and a symbol serving only to illuminate Jesus' gracious character, not her own identity. Of course Jesus was good and crucial to her. But first she mattered to herself. Whatever self-loathing and abasement may be inferred from her groveling treatment of Jesus, some tenacious tendril of self-respect must have moved her into his presence and emboldened her to risk the Pharisee's disgust. He may be seen as a version of the book of Proverbs' patriarch, the damning judge who sees human beings, especially women, as either virtuous or vile.

The city woman seems not to see herself so simplistically. And Jesus, sitting in for God at the Pharisee's table, can see what a wonderful mess she is, a woman with means and nerve, remorse and hope. The forgiveness he confers on her does not dehumanize her into stereotypical goodness. Jesus' declarations, "Your sins are forgiven; your faith has saved you," acknowledge that she is responsible for both her brokenness and her wholeness in relation to God. His charge to her, "Go in peace," seems less an ethical imperative concerning her future conduct than an affirmation of her present blessed integrity. Like its English language equivalent, *peace*, the biblical Greek word εἰρήνην (*eirene*), with which Luke ends the city woman's story, means freedom from conflict or war. The city woman is now free to go on with her life no longer at war with herself. Her purpose henceforth is not to overcome her immorality and curry divine favor by good behavior. Her task is to get up off the floor and live as though God, loving all of her and not just the "good" parts, can be counted on to continue to encourage her faithfulness, and in mercy to correct her when she fails.

I had some growing up and some failing to do.

My mother took me to garage sales to buy furnishings for my first apartment. She stood crying on the front porch as my father pulled out of the driveway hauling a trailer crammed with my stuff. I would be turning eighteen in a couple of weeks. Energized, I sat beside my father in the front seat of the packed car, sensing that my mother wanted me to grieve as she was grieving the departure of her youngest child. I now appreciate the emotional import of the moment for my mother as well as my father's workmanlike approach to getting me settled into an apartment. Back then I could not have been more pleased to be leaving home, setting out for a life of my own in the city of Chicago, where I enrolled in college.

Gideon and I no longer enjoyed each other's company. He returned to Paris. As it turned out, Chicago without a steady boyfriend to offer me safe haven was a hard and loveless place. It wasn't easy to make friends at school because the university, centrally urban and chiefly intended for commuter students, offered very little community life. Its campus, a grim, architectural folly with structural flaws and a Soviet appearance, discouraged relationships except of a brief, utilitarian sort.

Others knew the city differently, but I knew it as a paved concentration of individuals who could not and would not care for one another. Before long I was doing what I had learned to do when turned loose in Rome: take up with any man, many men, whose indiscrimination suited mine. My memories of the time blur grayly like the scenery through the windows of an elevated downtown train. Here a screech, there a jostle and a swerve, sustained monotony and then a stop, an exit at the same destination as before, the place of embarkations and untransformed returns.

Academically, my task, I had decided, was to write, so I majored in English. I took pleasure in writing stories and poems that exercised some literary promise and showcased my increasingly despairing worldview. I started failing courses outside my major, either because I refused to see their significance, or I stopped attending classes and neglected formally to withdraw from them. The more I wrote, the less I cared to study. I found it hard to concentrate on academics, to locate an internal self that could focus, take in information and synthesize ideas. Writing, however, mitigated the anonymity that seemed poised at all times to erase me. Writing confirmed and grounded me even when disappearance and dissociation were my chosen literary themes. After I had written, I could see the produce of my mind on a page, and there was something to that, something to consider and even prize. My lines of poetry and prose bore material witness to my innermost life, whether or not anyone else knew or cared about it. I knew. I cared. I began to live for this.

I came to understand it was not *having* written that gave me life. It was writing, the active experience of language, invention, description, and elaboration, the musicality of words mingling with each other. As people need to do whether they manage it or not, words congregated. They formed a community of meaning and sound. Feeling energetically connected to a life source, I would write. Marveling at what I had made, I would read and reread a nearly finished poem or story, adjusting punctuation, replacing one word with another more precise and rhythmic word. I would revise my writing for the sake of craft and to fulfill my need to keep on wording for myself what I had no one to hear me speak aloud. The writing process became to me roughly what the Lord's Prayer had been to the little girl who whispered it from memory under the covers. I addressed the darkness, broke into its long silence and discovered writing to be a confidant who took me wholly as I was, no questions asked and certainly none answered.

CHAPTER
4

Storied, Brief, and Sisterly

I wanted an answer. The silence that followed writing too closely resembled the feeling of being ignored. Loneliness and longing for connection set me searching for attention and appreciation as a writer, which is different from the quest for an interested reader. The former search tends to be narcissistic in nature, whereas the latter can be literary and connective, more generous than egoistic. Writers get into relationship trouble when we treat our works as currency of our own making and spend it on people in exchange for their admiration and affection. Like the money we pay, the love we get is counterfeit.

I attained the notice of my writing teacher, a first-time novelist the same age as Gideon. My alternative high school teachers had behaved honorably, teaching us ethics and generally boosting students' sense of self-worth. I was still looking for such encouragement from an appropriate role model. Without fully understanding it, I had now entered the new and harsh world of a large urban public university, where an adjunct creative writing instructor was unlikely to serve as the mentor I needed. He was the father of two small children to whose mother he was unhappily married, or so I concluded from his pursuit of me, the fascinated protégée. The writing teacher's fine hair smelled lemony, and he wore contact lenses rather unsuccessfully. He was always batting his eyes.

During a rendezvous at a neighborhood pub where underage people like me rarely drank (and so I was not carded), I asked my teacher what we become when we die.

"Worm meat."

I received his response as though I had wanted to hear it. Internally, deeper down than my effort to be cool with this coolest of all creatures, a published book author, I concealed my desire to be warmed and spiritually nurtured, which, of course, is what had prompted my question. I hid from myself the fact that I wanted the writing teacher to teach me something worth learning: that there is a greater life than this one we were living in which people lied to a spouse, fooled around with a student or a teacher, called it a good time and called it a night.

It was 1983. *Time* magazine named the computer Machine of the Year. Its cover pictured a colorless man sitting before a boxy monitor. Though he appeared to be considering two rising yellow lines on an onscreen graph, I could see he was not rising but dying, turning to plaster, drifting out of himself the way I too was incrementally dissociating from my body and vaporizing for lack of warmth and love.

Yet it was thrilling, an accomplishment, I thought, to have attracted the writing teacher. I bragged about our illicit romance to a classmate. He was an emotionally unstable young man who once had presented to the writing class a rape fantasy story in which the central character's name was the same as the teacher's. Did I imagine this young man would keep my dirty secret? Naively, I did. Did I imagine driven by jealousy he would telephone the writing teacher's wife and tell her everything? I did not, but this is what he did. Soon the writing teacher called me in a cold fury to tell me I was a dumb bitch and hang up.

He misspoke. I was not dumb but inexperienced at adultery, a practice in which secrecy is paramount. I was not a bitch, either, if by this word the writing teacher meant I was mean as an angry Rottweiler. Here was a desperate man, found-out and lashing out with the blunt instrument of misogyny, all that was left to him now that his cover was blown. Before this, in lust and the neediness common to writers, he had transmuted his hatred of women into all the charm it took to seduce an eighteen-year-old. I was just intellectually gifted enough to be interesting over a beer yet deficient enough in self-respect to mistake his sexual predation for affection. The fun was over now. He would move on to less troublesome conquests. I would move deeper into self-loathing.

How long, O Lord? How long until the girl got up?

You've heard the expression "touching bottom"?

You've heard, *was crucified, died and was buried; descended into hell.*

We're not there yet. Spiritually, I would have to go down there, to the depths of the hell we create here on earth, to the rock bottom where worms eat the meat of the dead, before rising up would become possible for me, and by no power of my own.

On the third day; rose again.

We're not there yet.

About the crucifixion I underwent and the hell I inhabited from ages eighteen to twenty-two, I could tell you tawdry stories. I could dig up and narrate memories of debauchery and debasement. We could have a real vestment ripper on our hands.

To recount literally some of the experiences in question would turn this book into trash. Reading it would make you bear witness to sin that need not be detailed to be understood. Parading and gawking are not our purposes. This is not reality TV. I offer selected personal stories and withhold others with the parabolic purpose of pointing toward God in the lives of women, contemporary and biblical. Many women's lives, like my own, have included times during which, at best, the kingdom of God lay dormant, buried, fruitless as an ungerminated seed, missing as a lost gold coin. I see the first twenty-two years of my life as a long underground sojourn almost entirely devoid of holy light. In the second half of those twenty-two years, I lived at high risk, the subject and the object of personal transgressions to which I limit my allusions here both to preserve privacy and to distinguish this work from entertainments that uncritically depict the erotic exploitation and violation of women.

By intuitive feel, I am writing my way into a space where honesty interacts with discretion, truthfulness with dignity, personal remembrance with biblical texts, poetry with prose, and feminism with Christian faithfulness. In blending life stories, Scripture, theology, and poetry, I am writing a kind of book I have not often read, for which the models are disparate and partial, derived from multiple literary genres that tend not even to be shelved together, much less contained within a single title. My point here is not to congratulate myself for originality or genre-bending, but to admit I find my task complicated and challenging. I am not interested in simplifying or tidying it because I am neither simple nor tidy, myself. I never met a woman who is, in Scripture or in life, and I would like to be faithful to both.

For women, Scripture and life entail love, fulfillment, peace, and joy the journey toward which is sometimes downright crucifying. Life comes by way of loss, resurrection by way of the cross. I persist in creating this cruciform memoir because I'm driven Godward and I want to write the risen life as I know it. I mean to be true to life without indulging in gratuitous "passion" narratives that revel in ecstasy or agony as though these were virtues.

The empty cross may assist me. The bloodied corpse has been removed from it. The cross remains in place, a reminder of betrayal, injustice, and torture but not perpetually laden with their images. The body removed from the empty cross is, of course, that of a man, Jesus. As a victim of the brutal form of capital punishment reserved for socially lowly subjects of the Roman Empire, Jesus entered, body and soul, into the degradation suffered by women and slaves. Even so, I find the empty cross to be a more helpful metaphor for women's struggle and transformation than a crucifix in all its gendered literality.

When shame and depression so influenced my daily decisions that I routinely treated my body like refuse, I still wrote poems. I managed to order words despite my inner chaos. I also enrolled in a college course on The Bible as Literature, telling myself it behooved me as a writer to develop a working acquaintance with this important literary text. Then I dropped out—of the course and of the university—in the middle of the midterm exam. Insofar as I had read the stories of the Pentateuch, I had not absorbed or understood them. The test questions seemed trivial and were certainly impossible for me to answer rightly. With a sensation of both defeat and liberation, I quietly closed my hefty New English Bible while my classmates kept hunching over their exam booklets. I tiptoed from the classroom avoiding the professor's gaze, my uncompleted exam jammed into my backpack with the useless three-pound book of unintelligible Scriptures.

Now I was no longer a writing student. I was just a writer, and there was some dignity and purpose to that. A constructive urge would take hold of me while I rode busses and worked crummy jobs. I would steal any available time and scrap paper to labor over a poem, a small artwork in the deeming that would awe me with its seeming will to be made and its unaccountable goodness. By "goodness" I don't mean literary finesse (these were the early scribbled works of a developing writer, after all). I mean I found in the works of my mind and hand the inherent, mysterious value that a living creature embodies, evoking reverence from its beholder. The word "poetry" is rooted in the Greek word ποιέω (*poeio*), which means "to make." Writing poetry was an act of creation. This much was good to me when little else seemed to be.

During the lonely city months after leaving my parents' home, I moved from apartment to apartment, job to job, and developed skills in the craft of making poems. These skills served me well a decade or so later, during my formal theological education. When the historical-critical approach to Scripture favored by my seminary professors did little to inflame my heart for God, I would apply their scholarly method to the subject matter of poems I was now moved to write about biblical women. I would learn what I could about ancient Near Eastern cultures and customs and bring this knowledge to bear in poems imagining the experiences of such scriptural figures as Rahab, Hannah, Tamar, and Miriam. In writing about (or *as*) these women, I would also draw on the experiences and emotions I had weathered as a younger woman in a society where female sexuality, power, spirituality, and intelligence continued, in many sectors, to be viewed with distrust and contempt.

Having closed the literary Bible at age twenty, I opened the historical, holy Bible in my thirties. Learning about the ancient cultures, patriarchal and frequently violent, in which biblical women made their way, I inevitably reopened personal memories of violation and humiliation. I sought redemption for all women by writing the poems that follow. They are not autobiographical, but are personal, prayerful, and infused with female cruciform experience and knowledge.

Your reading of them will be much enriched by your first reading the Scriptures they reference. Now I see how the poems vibrate with female rage and reverence. I honor the poet who wrote them. I celebrate the person she became. I love the God who can take a crucified woman by the mind and give her words of life.

A Bible Harlot (after Joshua 2:1-24)

A Bible harlot
works the naked, ancient present.
She walks the streets between survival
and salvation, making little of their difference
and fewer coins. If she makes it
to the morning ritually unstoned,
she sees herself as her own savior
and stops looking for the One
her holy clients dread.
Sated and ashamed, they slither from her bed
to offer up atoning sacrifices:
a hand laid on a bull's head,
a blade in its throat,
and the drama of sanctifying gore
restores a man to God,
but not his prostitute, who labors on,
beyond redemption.
Excepting Rahab,
Jericho's walled-up hooker,
genius of her own salvation.
She's working her family out of debt
when Joshua's two spies sneak by.
They like the way Rahab's window opens
to the milky, honeyed land of Canaan,

bordered by the Jordan, entered
through lush Jericho, city of palms.
They act more like horny bandits
than undercover operatives; they're spied
darkening her door.
The local king,
who prefers his subjects taxed and slavish,
is alerted to the hostile infiltration
and forced to beg for evidence and answers.
Rahab's all innocence and lies
and sends his loyal henchmen up the river
while her guests drowse on her rooftop,
concealed by rustling heaps of drying flax.
She's entertained enough politicos and priests
to know a holy martial power is poised
to smash the very walls that house her
before slaughtering toward Bethlehem
and all those promised lands.
Rahab's choices: Yahweh or a highway to damnation,
conversion by terror or a rope to hang herself.
She hangs it, instead, out that opportune window,
so the spies, having crept from their flaxen beds,
can slide, burning-palmed, out of town.
Rahab knows their safety lies
in hills voluptuous with shadows.
She commissions them to run and hide,
then dangles all her faith from one red thread,
the spies' parting gift to her of raveling assurance:
when warriors encircle Jericho
to demolish its walls with a shout of God's great name,
they'll see the blood-colored braid and know
Rahab is one whore worth saving.

Tomorrow, Tamar (after 2 Samuel 13:1-22)

Millennial pilgrims pour from the bus.
    Black cameras, the heavy pendants of memory
    swing from their necks.

The prayerful tourists shoot Jerusalem's sunlit streets
    and bobbing, bearded devotees facing the
                shadowy wall.

When they can,
    the tourists also shoot women,
    those masked and furtive Muslim mysteries
    who glide, legless, it seems, and silent
    at the elbows of their men.
On film, as in Western eyes, the women,
    hurrying home with sacks of chickpeas and mint
                leaves
    appear as veiled blurs, featureless and out of reach,

yet thickly visible,
unknown and unforgettable

as you, Tamar. Peace be upon you.
The peace you never knew in ancient days.

Like Noah's crow, soaring
    ragged and alone above earth's second chaos,

you disappeared without dying—

    a swallowed episode
in God's beautiful, violent book.

I look for you through green bus-glass in Jerusalem's
                streets,
    the bright, ugly avenues we pass en route
    to holy sites your shame would never let you near.

When I hear the muezzin's call to prayer,
    beckoning and mournful as the shofar,
    and see Allah's thousands with their foreheads in
        the dust,

Tamar, I remember
    the animal howl of your voice,
    your violated body in a torn gown
    outside your brother's bolted door, your forehead
    smeared with ash.

                                    You wandered

bleeding through Jerusalem,
    blamed for the lust of Amnon, your brother,
    prince of rapists and first-born, unpunished son
        of your father:

                            David, a king's king.

Second Samuel never says you died.
So I make my pilgrimage for you, Tamar, who must
        still be wandering this city,

your two millennia of suffering unavenged by
        Scripture.

Let me recollect you. Let me remember your life—
    storied, brief, and sisterly.

Let me stop for a supper of falafel, fried like the last
        meal you cooked,
    and gather the strength to keep looking for you,
    and pray that I'll find you
    somewhere in Jerusalem,

                    tomorrow, Tamar.

Midrash for Hannah (after 1 Samuel 1:1-20)

What you have to give
is birth. The history of God
is a trajectory of sons.
You've borne none. Year by year,
you follow the journeying families
and observe the encircling arms
of mothers as they carry
infants toward the Lord.
Running boys,
their bodies wild with energy
not yet circumscribed by law,
rush the pilgrimage to Shiloh,
as though speed were its own end,
as though worship were more
than habitual insult.

His other wife is waiting there,
his unimaginative Peninah,
with her tired provocations
and her brood. And he's there,
serving you a bowl of food,
a double portion of the meat
of consolation,
so much pungency and grease.
Your mouth locks like the womb
shut inside you by God
and so hollowed by time
that your love for Elkanah
is reduced to unproductive sex,
and eating and drinking
just perpetuate your emptiness.

Enter it, this grief,
this temple God has hidden
in the lives of barren women
and offer up the pure prayer
of your tears. Here,
the priestless sanctuary
of your desire is open;
here you're free to pour forth
the sacrificial logic of your heart,
to drive your silent bargains
so hard your lips tremble

and speak you back to the world
that takes you for a drunk
when you have never been so lucid,
so sure. But now you can tolerate derision
as well as vague, official blessings.
Now you must eat and ready your body
for the want that began
as your hollowness and closure
to be hallowed,
consummated by the Lord in you.

Miriamic Hymn (after Exodus 15:20-21)

How can I sing to you?
My throat goes silent
in wonder at your name,
which far outreaches the range
of my voice.
Yet because I must sing, I do.
I move from wordlessness to language,
true to my humanity:

you have made me
a creature of speech.
Accept this, my offering
of metaphors: these
are the horses of my journey
toward you. Without you,
I am a rider misguided by echoes
torn loose of their source
and diminishing.
This is a cry of broken being:
I have ridden to the sea,
and have drunk of its salt,
and I thirst. To quench me,
to cleanse me,
you must drown me first.
Yet this water is suffused
with your breath;
you will not allow its depths
to silence me forever.
You listen for the terms
of my sorrow,
then turn them
to the song of your praise.
Its lyric becomes
beautiful in my mouth.
It is for you
that I sing, and by you
that I am raised.

5

The Word Was God

Not long after I dropped out of college, my parents dropped me off in Paris on their way to a few other European destinations. No one having come along to replace Gideon, or me, he and I rendezvoused in the Latin Quarter. Parisians never took him for an American, so at ease was he with them and their language. Perhaps he never really had been an American, but a resident alien twice removed from the American mainstream, first by his Amish identity, secondly by his excommunication from that community of outsiders. He was now a fluent expatriate, as effortlessly able to take me to the radiant places every visitor to Paris must see as to art house cinemas, storefront galleries, and parties you would only attend as the guest of a local. I employed every last word of the French vocabulary I had learned in grammar school, every verb form I could summon, and even managed to converse with a friend of Gideon's about the roles of women in our respective cultures. "You are ahead of us," he told me. "French women envy you."

"The French like to have an American around," another man said to me at a dinner gathering. "It makes us feel more French."

I watched the host plunge her hands into a pan full of rock salt and extract a beautifully roast bird. I drank a lot of red wine that night. Gideon and I stumbled back to my hotel, past a street chanteuse aping Edith Piaf. She had pathos and vibrato going for her. "This is nice," I announced, "but Paris reeks of piss."

The next day I had a headache like an anvil to the cranium and blood in my urine: a hangover and a urinary tract infection, side effects of this last gasp, this lesser thing than a honeymoon. My parents came back through Paris, and we four dined at a restaurant Ben Franklin had frequented. Over fish soup, Gideon spoke of the time he and a friend flipped a coin to decide who would hire the one-armed prostitute soliciting them both. Gideon had lost his Amish morals, you see, but not his Amish candor.

We visited Chartres and Notre Dame. Both churches left me literally cold with their soaring stone insides buttressing illusions. An airport is no cathedral, but it may be a low-slung chapel of sorts, a way station through which pilgrims pass on their journeys. In the Charles de Gaulle airport I said goodbye to Gideon for the last time and boarded a plane back to the city where I was determined to make it as a writer.

Several months later in Chicago, I met a young Jew, an art school graduate, a marathon runner, good to his mother. Having foresworn men altogether, as frequently stood-up, finally fed-up women will do, I encountered Daniel when I was not looking for him, or for anyone like him or unlike him. I was arriving home from work one day, wheeling my bike into the apartment building when he introduced himself as my neighbor down the hall, saying he had heard I was a writer. I wondered if this meant the clacking of my typewriter had disturbed him (writers still composed on typewriters in those days). I wheeled my bike into the building and hoisted it onto my shoulder to haul it up four flights of stairs to my studio apartment. I had also sworn off roommates.

The doctor whose phones I answered by day had his own day job at another clinic. He had hired me to sit by myself, scheduling evening appointments in the office where moonlighting helped him pay his medical school bills. When the office phone was quiet, and after dark in my studio apartment with its view of the streetlit bricks next door, I wrote stories and poems, a few of which were published in local zines. Once or twice when my typewriter ribbon ran dry and the stores were closed, I snuck back into the doctor's office after hours to bang out my moody pieces on the hulking, humming IBM Selectric.

Daniel may have been more interested in the idea of a writer girlfriend than in me or my actual fiction and poems. Therein life was a plotless postmodern bitch and then you died pointlessly with style. I was more interested in the experience of writing than in Daniel, though he was better company than my solitude when I was not writing. *Lead me on a level path*, my thoughts chanted every morning to no one I believed in (Ps 27:11). Lead me to something, to someone; I beseeched any set of qwerty keys I could get my hands on, feeling for the words, putting them in sequences to make the yearning bearable by singing it in my mind and beating it out. Daniel, neither my light nor my salvation but my companion for a time, liked that I loved writing. He bought me a typewriter he could not afford. He cleared my path of rocks, leveled it a little, preceding me into our twenties.

I attended my first Seder at Daniel's mother Tania's home. She collected people, some of them just this side of homeless, who had no place else to go. There were bitter herbs and sweet spices, a ragtag assemblage of guests at Tania's table. Daniel managed a bit of Hebrew, sounding out the words like a boy at his bar mitzvah. A chair stood empty for Elijah, just in case. I appreciated Tania's blend of Seder custom and improvisation. The barbecued chicken's glossy sauce was as sweet as the Mogen David we drank.

Daniel's father, an African American physician neither Jewish nor present, had never married Tania nor even lived with her, though he had turned up now and then in Daniel's childhood. Not unlike Gideon before him, not unlike me, Daniel struggled with the neglected child syndrome that leaves a person unsure who he is. Daniel's skin was tawny, his hair dark and wavy. Physically he identified more closely with the Puerto Ricans in his neighborhood than with either of his parents. His fake Spanish sounded pretty good but didn't mean anything.

Daniel did jobs around the local Jewish college, but he never went to temple, never seemed to want to. I would have gone there with him if he had asked me to.

"Or let's try a different religion," I suggested. "It doesn't have to be Jewish."

"Try Jah love."

"I don't think I'm Rastafarian. I'm serious. How about Buddhism? Should we try that?"

"I don't know," Daniel said, and we didn't.

When the phone wasn't ringing in the doctor's office, I sometimes tried to heal my uneasy self by reading a book about women and self-esteem, yellow-highlighting passages that pretty well described my life. Unable to afford anything else, I attended psychotherapy appointments at a cheap community clinic staffed by psychology students. My mother, having recently completed her bachelor's degree, was now pursuing a master's in counseling. One day she mentioned to me that a classmate of hers, having recognized my mother's last name, had said she knew me and wanted nothing but the best for me. Not long after this, I disclosed to this same therapist my latest lousy decision, some infraction of the heart involving a guy I had allowed to become too important in my life. The therapist began openly weeping, so disappointed was she with my psychological progress. In reality I had begun to figure out a thing or two. For example, I decided this tearful session would be my last with her.

Writing was always there for me, loyal, patient, and lively. By writing I practiced creative attention. Thoughts and feelings presented themselves to my awareness and took on the bodies of words. Words related, quick to find other words to mingle with, making meaning and music. I discovered who I was and what I meant by sensing sentences that wouldn't tell me their full meaning until all their words were said. Sentences possessed the power to beget. Laying down one line of words would generate another. The papery void that previously had seemed to represent my own unworth would fill with language it well-pleased me to compose. But writing did not entirely fulfill me because however beautiful the words, they emptied out into a God-emptied world where beauty was a decoration and finally there were no objects worthy of devotion.

I saw vestigial devotion in Moscow, another great city I visited with my mother, at age twenty-one, when my father didn't want to go. Outside St. Basil's onion-domes in the rain, crusty Russian widows lined up. *Glasnost* was underway. This meant tourists, busloads of middle-class Western gapers, were given precedence of entry into the cathedral over ancient Orthodox ladies to whom the Politburo had nothing to prove. The *matushkas* with their gaudy umbrellas could wait while the Americans filed past to see the museum of icons. It was all too much for me, this bureaucratic disrespect for dutiful, deluded old women, uncomplaining, smelling of cabbage. I staged a private boycott, stomping off to GUM, the department store across Red Square. I bought a hammer-and-sickle-stamped paperweight and missed the tour bus back to the hotel.

Outside the Kremlin, I found taxis to be surprisingly scarce. Pedestrian tunnels underlie Moscow's immense boulevards. Pacing one tunnel, panic nearly closing off my throat, I finally stopped a guy wearing an Oakland Swimming T-shirt, hoping he might speak enough English to help me find a cab. I refused to sell him my red Reeboks (what would I have worn then? hideous Soviet vinyl slip-ons?). I gave him some dollars, and he led me to a strangely obscure taxi stand on a street I might never have found on my own.

Back at the hotel, I found my mother morosely spooning her borscht in the dining room with the other members of our tour group. Color leapt to her cheeks when she saw me, her prodigal daughter.

"You understand," I told her as she embraced me. "I couldn't go ahead of those poor old women."

"You scared me," she said into my shoulder (being a few inches shorter than I). "The bus driver insisted we leave. I was out of my mind with worry."

I told her about Oakland Swimming, and she laughed.

"Those years on the swim team paid off."

That night, I went to the hotel's basement pool. Underwater lights embedded in the pool walls faintly lit the otherwise dark deck. A female attendant, burly and somber, handed me a towel. She was the sole person present as I slipped into the wobbly, luminous water. Submerged, I laughed at the unintended adventure of my day, the strange privileges and trials of travel. Silvery bubbles of breath escaped me and rose. I found my heart quickening, a breathless thrill rising inside me. I burst through the surface, gasping and blinking in the dark, treading water.

What, for a poet, can it mean to "make it as a writer"? In Chicago I reenrolled in the college I had left two years earlier and resumed majoring in English with an emphasis on creative writing. I also performed much better than I previously had done in required nonmajor courses. To the reading and writing of poetry, I brought a zoomed-in intensity of focus that excited me and marginalized such concerns as how I might eventually go about earning a living.

Across from me in Intermediate Writing of Poetry sat a fine-boned young man our professor nicknamed The Surgeon for his incisive, unsentimental editing of other students' works. Unlike The Surgeon, who tactfully handed classmates their poems with entire stanzas crossed out, I was a class bigmouth, opining on everybody's writing and turning in lots of poems of my own. A few showed linguistic precision and nerve, but I received no feedback on them from The Surgeon.

Somehow (*somehow*) I had gravitated to the seat beside him. One day after class, as other students dispersed, I turned to him with my characteristic subtlety and asked, "How come you don't amputate my poems?"

"I like your poems," The Surgeon said, the first words he ever spoke to me directly. He and I have been married for well over twenty years now. I still swoon a little at the thought of the first four words he said to me, especially the word *like*, the way he emphasized it to explain himself and contain something more than literary admiration, the way it made a verbal bridge between *I* and *your*, the way *poems* meant *writing, mind, soul, heart, nearness, scent,* and everything.

Had I not dropped out of college, had I not returned to college two years later, I would not have met The Surgeon, who is not in fact a medical professional but an academic two years my junior, named Ken. He is also a Presbyterian, the son of a preaching woman, and was a churchgoer at twenty when I met him.

I thought the churchgoing was something Ken should outgrow as one might a distaste for fresh vegetables. Fortunately for me, Ken did not think I should shape up and get religion, and never sought to convert me. He was much more respectful of my atheism than I was of his faith, which I envied without knowing it and sometimes ridiculed. He possessed the self-respect to tell me to knock it off. I did knock it off, love having thunderstruck me and replaced the clenched fist inside me with a heart.

The Voice That Is Great Within Us. It's a beautiful phrase and an anthology of twentieth-century poetry. A paperback brick crammed with mostly mid-century writing, it was the sole textbook assigned for the writing class in which I met Ken. Its title comes from a line in Wallace Stevens's "Evening without Angels." The poem typifies Stevens's humanism, his irreligious outlook. It also points to that of our teachers and the writers they felt were best for our impressionable intellects and the writing we would produce, piles of which they would have to read.

In the academic literary world, the word was God alright, but by no means in the divine, originary sense of λόγος (*logos*, Word) that John the Gospel writer means when he says "the Word was God" (1:1). Words were sonic, inky names for tangible things outside of which no ideas mattered and no supernatural intelligence existed. This according to the modernist poetics of William Carlos Williams, whose plainspoken, imagistic poems our teachers encouraged us to emulate. I had trouble doing so because I was roiling with feeling, and that too was discouraged.

"If you're writing and you feel an emotion coming on," said one of our poetry professors, "go make coffee." Keep your writing clean and spare, like a room in which Ernest Hemingway might feel at ease.

The decidedly masculine voice our teachers considered great was not in fact within about half of us. We were women, and as such, some of us perpetrated what one professor called "mean man poems," impassioned embarrassments in the vein of Sylvia Plath, Anne Sexton, and Sharon Olds. Much preferred were the precise, observant verses of a woman like Elizabeth Bishop, who had the good taste to leave her depression, alcoholism, and homosexuality out of her work, which was relatively scant, perfectionism having kept her from proliferating.

One of our teachers did approve of Diane Wakoski's poetry, which surprised me because it was rife with mean men and female feeling. At a used bookstore I paid five dollars for a paperback copy of Wakoski's *Inside the Blood Factory*, her third poetry collection. Reading it, I felt as I once had felt upon finding a cameo brooch set in rose gold among the heaped costume jewelry in a thrift store. This book was a treasure, unique and overlooked. As I read Wakoski's self-referential, personally mythological poems, I understood: women's strong words—including those, like Wakoski's, concerning abandonment, betrayal, and rejection of women by men—could articulate experience and vision as worthy literarily as the impersonal and secular writings of the male poets I was being schooled to imitate.

There were no women among the university's writing faculty. Nor did the several tenured poets and fiction writers ever discuss the writing process during their workshops. They emphasized mechanics, technique, and critique. Students' writing lives were oddly divorced from our participation in the university writing community, as though our reasons for making poems and crafting stories, our experiences of creativity, language, and expression were too intimate and messy for academic consideration. What mattered was the betterment of the works we produced. How we produced it, who we were, what we felt and believed were of little interest.

A student writer would bring enough paper copies of a poem or short story to distribute to each other student and the teacher of a writing workshop. When your turn came around, you would gulp, read your piece aloud, then endure the cavernous silence that invariably followed. It would eventually be broken, often by a faultfinding remark and other spoken opinions, positive and negative. Ostensibly this ego-stripping exercise would help people write well. While the writing work-shops heightened my attentions as a reader and my editorial acumen, they seemed to involve only a select function of my brain, the part I would have utilized if assembling a cuckoo clock, striving for sturdy construction, temporal accuracy, a modicum of decoration, and pleasingly mimetic birdsong.

Against our professors' recommendations, I stashed a copy of *Ariel* in my backpack. I marveled at Sylvia Plath's lethal diction as I made my lurching way aboard a bus or train to campus or my latest part-time job. I did not identify with Plath's psychotic outlook on everything from a knife-knicked thumb to a honeycomb. I could see she took it, or it took her, too far. But her way with words, all defiant incantation, woke me up like espresso. She dared me to write poems that clacked and swore and attacked their subject matter with the energy of the young woman I was: a strong-willed writer finished keeping quiet. It was just this bold, emerging poet with whom Ken fell in love. In a poem of his own, he compared the effect of my writing to that of a stiletto. As if to prove his point, he gave me the gift of an actual antique stiletto wrapped in a scrap of cowhide.

After the semester ended, Ken and I founded a writers' group. Our small gang of young poets would meet in one another's apartments to drink wine and coffee and practice the writing life without supervision or evaluators. During the first summer of the group's ten active years, at age twenty-two, I composed a rather hallucinatory poem that moved from the profane to the sacred, exorcising in between the voice within me that was love-desperate, self-hating, God-haunted, yet perhaps also great. The poem languished for two years in the backlog of a literary journal's accepted submissions. Finally it appeared in print, eventually to be read by the poet Charles Simic, who selected it for inclusion in *The Best American Poetry 1992.*

I Want to Marry You

I want to marry you.
I'm a fossil, perfectly preserved.
You could excavate me from the cold guts
of this tough jewel, could chip away
chunks and brush sharp dust
from my lips as I whispered, take me wholly,
make me whole.
Take me up to a high hot town.
In a room done in dry rough gold cleaned clean
I will gingerly rest my ass, test the bed for groans
                and gives.
You'll bring me fishy water in a glass.
I will drink it, I will lie
in foreign darkness, watch my feet
reach above the blue moving desert of your back
for the moon, from which I'll try
to wring a little honey.
Honey, sun will ring off rocks,
will sting us for a week or two.
Our life will be a slap, a sneeze.
Oh, how I'll wish you would put down
that magazine and look the hell at me.
But I will never take my dress off.
I will never take my dress off, the white one,
the right one, the holey lacy binding binding
tight one.
I will swim in stone again,
wearing my dress. I will emerge,
wetter than ever, wearing my best dress.
But your face will remain buried in the gloss

of pages, and I will bury myself
in fishy pool water
til I'm dredged from the depth of that juicy jewel
by another man who will not have managed
to save my life.
Stiff and dripping, dressed in white,
I will embrace the cooking, empty air.
In a new voice thick with love, you'll say,
Hey, mister, that's my wife you've got there.
But he will not hear you, he will be dancing
for me, for me. He'll dance a wild
shapeless dance, his unclean fist
bashing the skin of a shimmering tambourine,
his icy taps chiseling a random rhythm in the rock
for me. And honey,
his chaotic music will riddle me til
I'm half again the girl I used to be, til
I'm senseless, perforated ecstasy,
til I'm holy.

I write this book a full twenty years after the personally dazzling moment when my poetry kept one-time anthological company with the works of such luminaries as Adrienne Rich, Mary Oliver, and yes, Elizabeth Bishop. The *Best American Poetry* honor was flukish, unrepeatable, Cinderella-esque, but did not change my life. Change had come to me already, in the act of writing and in the strong love to which writing led me. I had been married to Ken for three years when I enjoyed my fifteen minutes of poetic fame.

Ken is not the "you" to whom the poem is addressed. Nor is he "another man" who appears in the poem. "You" and "he" are mythologized men in my life (here I borrowed a page from Diane Wakoski's poetics of personal mythology): desired, disappointing, and destructive, before love rolled away the stone that entombed the poem's speaker, an also-mythologized me. Hers is a crucified voice, asserting itself in a purgatorial croak to beg for salvation but not to claim any selfhood. Such female helplessness is the problem some feminists see as intrinsic to the relationship of women to Christ. Feminist though I was, the longing for a savior the poem expresses was more insistent in me than any image of personal political empowerment I might have wished to project.

Each poet represented in the *Best American Poetry* was invited to write remarks on his or her selected poem for inclusion in the book's appendix. I wrote, "In order to comment on the poem, I have to talk about love, which, I've learned, plunges us into our darkest histories and then brings us back up still breathing, with artifacts to show for ourselves. Or maybe we stop breathing when we're down there. Yes, I think we do, and then love, like God, revives us, and lets us keep our memories. My poem is a souvenir of that salvation, and addresses salvation itself, in ways that mystify and surprise me."

Love, like God. There is *like* again, that intervening word.

Several months after writing "I Want to Marry You," I was alone one afternoon. Late March was darkening Chicagoland. Ken had not yet come home from the tech support job he worked after classes. I enjoyed the lamps in our little apartment. They gave the rooms golden incandescence, as love had come to do in my life, gently burning through the gloom and replacing it with promise. I switched on the reading lamp beside the soft blue chair Ken had moved into the home we now shared. On an impulse twenty-two years in the making, I sat down and prayed.

I stammered and meandered and asked God just to be there, to watch me as I stumbled from bitter unbelief into faith. The blue chair, for all its comfort, was my Gethsemane. I had come to it in unplanned surrender, dreading abandonment, longing for release. Praying, I handed over all my effects and artifacts, personal memories and the hereditary histories I carried in my marrow. I offered up old countries, ancestral migrations, mother tongues and mother churches, fatherlands and massacres no one I knew could speak of even to God. I relinquished private ungrieved losses, wars and the wounds they inflict, the scars they leave on victims and victors alike. To the silence I dared hope was alive and strong enough to redeem godless me, at last I blurted, *Here.*

Of course I didn't know what I was doing. But this fumbling act of devotion expressed the same inchoate hunger that had driven me unwittingly in earlier years to partake of those bastardized communions that don't satisfy: the ritual passing of the burning joint from hand to hand; the shadow play and tribal beat of late night dance clubs; the grappling urgency of lovers who don't love one another.

I emerged blinking from the prayer, aware in a rudimentary but sure and certain way that my supplication had contained its answer. The answer was the same unhesitating *yes* that had been too deeply buried in my undercover childhood prayers for me then to understand. Now I understood. I believed. Dazed, I caught myself smiling at the question that occurred to me in the prayer's afterglow, though it was unclear who was asking whom: *What took you so long?*

What takes so long? What takes some of us so long?

I am a preaching woman and have been for several years. I am still young enough that many of my churchgoing listeners are one to three decades older than I am. They have been around long enough to have figured out much of what I speak about on Sundays. I believe they often know at some level of their beings what I say before I preach it. Preaching can bring into consciousness realities that dwell unrecognized in worshipers. The stories of their lives in God, their deaths and resurrections, are told in the pages of the Bible, but remarkably few of them read it. As a preacher I broadcast news to which worshipers have access in their souls and Scriptures, but these are the last sources many of them look to for insight.

What takes some of us so long to learn is that we have within us what we think we lack. In his preface to the Japanese edition of *New Seeds of Contemplation*, Thomas Merton writes, "Christians themselves too often fail to realize that the infinite God is dwelling within them." Merton's own early life reflected such a failure of realization.

In the pulpit I realize little that is new. But on a better Sunday, my preaching points to something ancient and precious in my congregants. Many reject or forget their intrinsic worth like a piece of fine jewelry tossed into a bin of plastic bracelets and beads. Because we assume little of value can be found within us, few of us bother to look. We fear we'll find in ourselves something so shameful or painful we decide it's better to keep busy than to be still and know God is God. It seems more prudent to make coffee than to reckon with a feeling. My task when I preach is to speak messages that mean, *Reckon with it. Look deeper into your life. Rummage around in the stuff you cast off. Read the book you closed long ago. In that old Bible story you doubt can tell you anything new, in that memory you have no further use for, God may be found. God will help you live your life with love, and God will help you die your death in peace.*

Human beings' frustrated efforts to manage our lives without holy help remind me of the tea parties my friends and I pantomimed underwater in the swimming pool as girls. We wriggled to keep our skinny bodies submerged at an imaginary table. We held invisible cups and saucers, shouting unintelligible pleasantries until our breath ran out. Sometimes I want to ask people, *Why do you work so hard to appear as if nothing's awry? Why is it so important not to hear what's being said to you? Wouldn't it be easier to breathe than hold your breath? Why not admit who you actually are?* Having practiced my share of fakery and subterfuge, I find truthfulness takes less effort. So when I preach and write I try to surface and say clearly what comes to me through my reading of the Bible, the world, and my heart.

The prayer I was given to pray at last while sitting in the blue chair had been in me all along, since even before my girlhood encounter with the great presence in the kitchen. The moment I reclaimed in adulthood the devotion I had attempted then disowned in childhood, I encountered the God I had given up on years before. When I preach or pray in public, and when I write a book, I reenact the same searching, speechifying instinct that finally led me to pray on that gray March afternoon. For me, wording made, and it makes, all the difference between spiritual exile and belonging to the maker of the world. The love of a human being made me capable of praying, and then, more than ever, love freed me to write.

We are created and beloved, accompanied and lingual, and it takes us—some of us—decades of loneliness, striving and suffering to know it, if we ever do. Until we come to know our true situation, that we are beheld and indwelled by One who gives us life, healing, help, and sustenance, we are spiritual strangers. We thrash around doing damage. We strain to understand lesser messages than God's and garbled ones at that. All this dispiriting struggle drowns out the Gospel we already know deep down, etched as it is in our inmost selves, retold as it is in the Bible.

We are people to whom a generative word once was spoken that still is life-giving. All speech and writing is secondary to an original language through which we are animated and can be illumined: "In the beginning was the Word, and the Word was with God, and the Word was God. He was in the beginning with God. All things came into being through him, and without him not one thing came into being. What has come into being in him was life, and the life was the light of all people" (John 1:1-4).

The prologue of John's gospel is a hymn to the Word that harkens back to Genesis. There God is the poet of all poets, the maker of all makers whose spoken ποίησις (*poeisis*) manifests day and night, water, sky and earth, sun, moon, stars, plants and creatures. Life comes into being through the Word who is God and is with God. Human beings, created as we are in God's own image, are endowed with power to realize things through speech and writing. In making poems as a young unbeliever, I tapped into an energetic verbal mystery without knowing it belonged to God. When I finally broke down and addressed the mystery directly, I heard my voice uttering a living word not of my own conceiving. I could no longer fail to realize God dwells within me as God dwells within everybody.

An hour or so after I got up out of the blue chair, Ken came home from work. Shyly, after dinner, I admitted, "I think I found God today."

I wanted to go to church, I told him, suddenly adamant and anxious. He had taken a break from churchgoing after heavy involvement in the emotionally fraught merger of two small Presbyterian congregations on Chicago's southwest side. We lived on the north side of the city and needed a church we could call our own. I flopped open the yellow pages. Because Ken was a reasonable Presbyterian and not some zealot with oppressive ideas about God and women, I decided we should visit the closest Presbyterian church to our apartment. We could get there by bus the very next Sunday, which would happen to be Easter.

So this was Holy Week. Not that I had ever heard of such a thing. Not that I possessed any conscious insight into the notable timing of my spiritual awakening by prayer. I had been to church exactly once, for the Roman Catholic wedding of a friend's sister, and knew nothing about the liturgical calendar. Perhaps in my city travels I had noticed a Lenten purple sash adorning a church door, or a posted Holy Week and Easter worship schedule. I have no recollection of an outward prompt that led me on that Holy Week afternoon to abandon my atheism and speak to God after many years of estrangement. A few days earlier, had a Palm Sunday *hosanna* escaped an untidy, joyous church processional, wafted on the wind and reached my ready ears? Had it made me wonder whom it honored?

If I had overheard anything, not my ears but my heart had perceived *hosanna* followed close behind by betrayal, fear, and doom. Each Holy Week these unholy terrors murmur and encroach like low thunder, as they must before Friday can properly embody its bloody goodness, Saturday its grave silence, Sunday its bright, shocking hope.

Ken respected the fact that prayer had abruptly altered me on the inside and was making new demands of me. I told a writer friend about my newfound desire to attend a Presbyterian church. "They believe in Jesus, you know," he said. "Have you considered the Unitarians?"

Undeterred, I got up early on Easter morning. Ken and I wore dressy clothes under our raincoats and leapt over puddles on our way to the bus stop.

As we arrived at our chosen Presbyterian church, my feet went cold, and I began to consider the Unitarians. Motley urban worshipers were assembling in a hundred-year-old building that seemed never to have undergone renovation. The varnish on the pews was gummy from humidity and age. The sanctuary floor sloped and creaked beneath decrepit carpet. Worst by far was the purple-on-white felt banner hanging from the ceiling, proclaiming, "He Is Risen!" as though any reasonable person could believe a thing like that.

Upon seeing the homely Jesus-y banner, my first thought was to bolt from the church. Despite my skeptical friend's warning, it had not occurred to me that Jesus, and him risen,

would figure prominently in this Easter Sunday service of
Christian worship.

Rank beginner. Remedial. The terms understate my status
as a churchgoer that day. To be a worship rookie was a misery
in light of this particular church's sparse attendance. There
was, as the old gospel lyric puts it, no hiding place down here.
I simply had to sit down in a pew overseen by the alarming
banner, in full view of all comers: toddlers, geriatrics, and a
few dozen adults apparently nonplussed by the resurrection
nonsense going on.

"He is risen indeed!" they replied in unison, according to
their printed programs. If they believed it, why did they need
scripts? It was bizarre collective behavior, made weirder by
the wanderings and yelps of random children too young to
sit still and read.

"I don't like this," I whispered to Ken in desperation.
"Can we go?"

"Hang in there." He squeezed my hand.

He had not warned me about the standing up, the sitting down, the standing up again, or, Lord have mercy, the
singing. To funereal accompaniment, the people stood and
warbled musty, ending-rhyming songs about death having
lost its sting, evidently unaware that this religious display
caused a stinging effect all its own. Then came the recita-
tion of a creed for which we were instructed to stand yet
once more and read a paragraph beginning "I believe." No
one had consulted us on our beliefs or asked us if we could
assent to this statement and its preposterous, bewildering
litany. *I believe in the resurrection of the body?* At that point
I quietly gave way to tears.

Eventually I came to love Christian worship, especially
the unpolished, imperfect kind where people let their glorious, ragged humanity show. But on this Easter morning
I was completely unprepared for such public sacred real-
ism. Though I felt conspicuous, fraudulent and foolish, two

anchorholds kept me in place throughout the service: Ken, warm and reassuring at my side, and the primly attired woman who was not the pastor but co-led the service from a lectern, lucidly reading from the Bible. She did not invite others to stand up or chime in, and for this I offered silent thanks.

I listened to the woman, comprehending her vocabulary and syntax but not the substance of the text she read. I sensed she understood it deeply, however. Without fanfare or theatrics, she reverenced the words she read. She demonstrated that the things I could not abide in what I supposed was typical Christian religion, especially its hostility to women, were not necessarily so. Here was a woman standing up in church, plainly speaking sacred language on a sacred day, and everyone but an ancient dozing gentleman and a baby or two was paying respectful attention. She appeared unself-conscious, conscious instead of something greater than herself. She seemed infused with calm dignity, as though the words she read were written inside her, and she was saying them by heart. She had in her the light and life I had come to church to find. Listening to her I wanted to speak as she spoke. Looking at her I wanted to shine like she shone.

CHAPTER
6

Give Me This Water

The girl stood at a sink of dishwater. The young woman sat like a lotus at dusk. Unbidden, then bidden, the living God was present. Could it be the girl was led to the water, the woman summoned to the liminal hour between day and night? Could it be she was cherished and chosen?

It could. We all are God's wanted children. Sacred significance is each one's birthright. Sooner or later, in a Christ-prepared heavenly room, the fearfully wonderful reflection will be shown. Even now, see your own mirrored face and know you were made good in secret, in waters that ripened your flesh. You emerged to reveal the maker's artistry. Know your story is written in a good book.

I detect in the stories of biblical women my own watercolor likeness.

Somewhere deep in the well of memory is submerged the name of a woman of Sychar, Samaria, who was led to the water and there encountered Jesus. She has had a profusion of partners but perhaps little love. She has hauled bucket upon bucket of water, but a thirst persists in her that nothing slakes. Day after day the sun rises, burns and rolls for hours overhead, then drops back down behind the edge of the horizon, and she goes on worshiping the unknown. She is the wrong ethnicity and gender for a respectable Jew to talk to at high noon in full view of her people and his, who do not customarily mix. Custom stops neither of them from discovering the other's beloved identity.

> A Samaritan woman came to draw water, and Jesus said to her, "Give me a drink." (His disciples had gone to the city to buy food.) The Samaritan woman said to him, "How is it that you, a Jew, ask a drink of me, a woman of Samaria?" (Jews do not share things in common with Samaritans.) Jesus answered her, "If you knew the gift of God, and who it is that is saying to you, 'Give me a drink,' you would have asked him, and he would have given you living water." The woman said to him, "Sir, you have no bucket, and the well is deep. Where do you get that living water? Are you greater than our ancestor Jacob, who gave us the well, and with his sons and his flocks drank from it?" Jesus said to her, "Everyone who drinks of this water will be thirsty again, but those who drink of the water that I will give them will never be thirsty. The water that I will give will become in them a spring of water gushing up to eternal life." The woman said to him, "Sir, give me this water, so that I may never be thirsty or have to keep coming here to draw water."
>
> Jesus said to her, "Go, call your husband, and come back." The woman answered him, "I have no husband." Jesus said to her, "You are right in saying, 'I have no husband'; for you have had five husbands, and the one you have now is not your husband. What you have said is true!" The woman said to him, "Sir, I see that you are a prophet. Our ancestors worshiped on this mountain, but you say that the place where people must worship is in Jerusalem." Jesus said to her, "Woman, believe me, the hour is coming when you will worship the Father

neither on this mountain nor in Jerusalem. You worship what you do not know; we worship what we know, for salvation is from the Jews. But the hour is coming, and is now here, when the true worshipers will worship the Father in spirit and truth, for the Father seeks such as these to worship him. God is spirit, and those who worship him must worship in spirit and truth." The woman said to him, "I know that Messiah is coming" (who is called Christ). "When he comes, he will proclaim all things to us." Jesus said to her, "I am he, the one who is speaking to you." (John 4:7-26)

Speaking to her amid her daily rounds, Jesus overturns the woman's empty vessel, disrupts her quotidian labor, and invites anyone who thirsts—including present-day women of all ethnicities—to drink deeply of life-giving water no one need go to extraordinary lengths to draw. Telling her marital history without condemnation, Jesus deems gospel the résumé of every woman's body and being.

Messianic revelation happens in holy diaspora every day. We all are chosen people and this is the Lord's day. No day we live is wasted time, no love we give, however unreturned or exploited, is lost to God. No one is unclean or unworthy of blessing, none disallowed to drink from the profound source of life.

The girl immersed herself in swimming pools. She dipped her hands in dishwater. When she whispered the Lord's Prayer she had scissored from a Christmas card, she joined her voice with those of a great cloud of witnesses whose alleluias rained from heaven to earth. She comprehended none of this. She worshiped what she did not know. Later, after she was sickened and sent away, she heard a man on the radio singing a wild river song, and she wanted to be taken to the water with him.

Where did the voice that was great within me go throughout the years I mistook God's silence for absence and angrily forsook my little faith? What became of my unsaid prayers during the long, lonesome season of my disbelief?

Until at last I prayed in the blue chair, faith and prayers lay crucified and buried in a cave in me, a stone grave. The unmourned, scarcely mentionable deaths in my parents' past haunted me. A secret sadness weighed me down inside that sometimes made me feel like a motherless child. When I listened for God's voice, instead I heard the muffled outcry of family history, like Jeremiah's prophecy for my namesake: "lamentation and bitter weeping. Rachel is weeping for her children" (Jer 31:15).

Children bear not only ancestral legacies bequeathed to them by intent or accident, but also archetypal stories that tell truths the human psyche knows despite all trivial pre-occupations and crucial forgettings. I forget the baby girl I was, but I know this: until I was a year old or so, my name was Rae. On my birth certificate, "Rae" is crossed out, and "Rachel" is written in my mother's hand. Who was Rae, and what became of her?

"Rachel," meaning lamb, evokes a vulnerable life. In *Songs of Innocence and Experience*, poet William Blake emphasizes the lamb's innocence, asking in a child's lyric, "Little lamb, who made thee?" The tender-voiced, softly clothed creature suggests to Blake not a sacrificial animal but the Creator-Christ who "calls himself a Lamb." Blake affirms, "We are called by His name," identifying Jesus with the children meant to learn God's love from this song. As a child who bore a lamb's name but never heard such a song, I was, to resort to the problematic idiom, the black sheep. I learned you make your own hell here on earth. I felt my life to be in jeopardy, my safety sacrificed.

Why, despite rejecting religion, did my mother rename me biblically? Did "Rachel" simply seem to sound more melodious and feminine than "Rae"? Was my mother unconsciously retrieving some shred of the Scriptures she had dismissed? Whatever may have been her reason for adding that second syllable to my first name, my early spiritual development if not my physical appearance resembled some attributes of biblical Rachel.

Establishing the pattern that John the gospel writer later modifies in his chronicle of Jesus' travels and encounters, the book of Genesis tells of a momentous encounter between a man and woman at a well: "Rachel came with her father's sheep; for she kept them. Now when Jacob saw Rachel, the daughter of his mother's brother Laban, and the sheep of his mother's brother Laban, Jacob went up and rolled the stone from the well's mouth, and watered the flock of his mother's brother Laban. Then Jacob kissed Rachel, and wept aloud" (Gen 29:9b-11).

Eventually, in Genesis, it will be Rachel who weeps. As her story develops, she embodies yearning, resentment, connivance, and heartache, features in which I see the semblance of my younger, thwarted self.

Rachel waits. She is made to wait years for marriage and children, the things meant to fulfill her, which they never quite do. When she is young and beautiful, love finds her at the water well, but Jacob must work seven years for Rachel's father, Laban, before he may marry his beloved. Laban then tricks Jacob into marrying Leah, Rachel's elder sister, and into seven more years' labor after Rachel becomes Jacob's co-wife with Leah, an arrangement fraught with rivalrous tension. True to biblical ideals of feminine fruitfulness, Leah gladly bears Jacob multiple sons, while Rachel must continue to wait, this time to conceive.

She becomes belligerent when she does not get what she wants. Envious of Leah's prolific fertility, Rachel demands Jacob give her children, threatening to die if he fails. She manipulates her maid and her sister alike in her struggle to become pregnant by Jacob. As soon as she has finally borne a son (and named him Joseph), Rachel becomes dissatisfied and greedy for another (Gen 21:29–30:24).

In an ancient world where women's worth and power depend entirely on men's provisions or caprice, Rachel embodies female shame, anxiety, self-interest, and victimhood. Over the course of three chapters in Genesis, she evolves from comely, compliant virgin to patriarchy's object, embittered and duplicitous. When her fortunes suffer as the result of competition between her husband and her father, Rachel angrily steals her father's household idols. What he has refused her, she takes from him and hides from her husband. Possession of such religious objects signifies their owner's status as a family leader and property owner. But Rachel is saved neither by the trickery with which she has seized economic power, nor by the societal respect conferred on her through the production of sons. Jacob, unaware his wife has purloined her father's household idols, bans all such gods, delegitimizing Rachel's stolen fortune. She soon dies in childbirth, naming her last baby Ben-oni, "son of my sorrow." Jacob denies Rachel the right to leave her son even this dubious maternal legacy, renaming him Benjamin, "son of the right" (Gen 31:14-16, 33-35; 35:2,16-20).

Rachel's last son bears names that reveal his mother's then his father's sense of themselves as sorrowful and righteous, respectively. At times I have been tempted to imagine that "Rae" briefly afforded me a sunshinier disposition, like a luminous ray, than I had as young Rachel. Life looked bright in the beginning but took a wrong turn, as though the name change changed me from a happy baby to a child of sorrow.

Wittingly or not our parents make decisions that imprint us with identities and memories, perhaps even callings and destinies. In my given name I hear possibility, grief, and hope. In the story of Rachel, my biblical namesake, I see millennia of women waiting and fighting for blessings that come late if they come at all. I see in Rachel women whose lives could be wellsprings of great creativity, yet whose depths go undiscovered, their potential outpourings stoppered by domestic exploitation and societal oppression. These women are driven into conflict with their sisters and fathers, their husbands and God. They visit sorrow on their children. Their legacy of lamentation and bitter weeping continues for many generations until God intervenes to promise the people's return to a place of solace, belonging, and fruition.

Sorrow is central to the only life story I can honestly tell. In adolescence the roles of the outcast and the captive were imposed on me by elders attempting to tame my wildness and govern my behavior, until they gave up such attempts altogether. Children need loving discipline lest they become unruly tyrants unable to practice self-control. Childrearing challenges parents not beset by trauma, grief, addiction, and all the hardships these imply. How much harder parenting must have been for my mother and father. When their youngest daughter angrily acted out the family unwellness no one was permitted to notice, they made me live locked among the mentally ill, wander the streets of an unfamiliar European city, and be schooled among delinquents. To recall, understand, and forgive these pivotal, definitive decisions is not to hush them up or excuse them but to glean blessings and learn lessons, unwanted yet redemptive, about family, girlhood, sanity, safety, and sorrow.

Who gets to deem some people crazy, foreign, or failures? Consider the labels, how they distort; they neither help nor heal. Consider the immigrant, the black sheep, the identified patient, the little girl lost, the lost cause, the loose woman, the names that determine who we think we are and whether we beam like a ray of sunshine or are led like a lamb to the slaughter.

In the fullness of time, my sorrow intersected with God's grace. The great, transformative gift of salvation lends my life and this book their cruciform character. The cross connotes evil overcome by love, suffering transformed into joy. Whereas biblical Rachel's lovely innocence turns into bitter experience, my own bitter life was saved and eventually sweetened by grace. I became convinced of God's reality and goodness. Unlike my namesake whose last word was sorrow, I vow mine will be "amen." I pray I will leave a sorry legacy to no one.

I mean for my life and this book to give praise, though not by the blithe optimism that sometimes passes for Christian faith. To write on the resurrection side of the cross is to remember crucifixion yet rejoice in utter newness that means more than unscathed naiveté ever could. I am both Rae and Rachel, both my parents' daughter and God's. I am also descended from a biblical matriarch who struggled, gave life, gave grief, suffered sorrow, and died. Rachel's bones lay entombed, silent for centuries. It takes Jeremiah, the Lord's persecuted, persevering oracle, to hear her grief and declare it redeemed. Jeremiah broadcasts the sorrow of exiles then announces its reversal, transmitting God's instruction and promise to the people: "Keep your voice from weeping . . . there is hope for your future, says the LORD: your children shall come back to their own country" (Jer 31:16-17).

Jeremiah's "book of consolation" (chapters 30 and 31) speaks chiefly to the scattered, captive people of Israel and Judah, in the sixth or seventh century BCE. Essential to Jewish identity though this context is, the Bible's meaning is not restricted to any select ethnic group, ancient past, or dominant gender.

Contemporary Christian women may derive hope from Jeremiah's prophecy. Circumstantially different from the hope that comforted God's people under Babylonian rule, our present hope is just as needed and real as theirs was long ago. If we understand ourselves to be Rachel's distant daughters, then the prophesied return home of her children can console us. This is provided we continue to redress the history of women's systemic banishment from many communities, including leadership circles in the very churches (our "own country") where God calls us to claim our wholeness in Christ.

Wherever women assent to remain marginal to the spirit and truth in which God is rightly worshiped according to Jesus, we decline to drink fully of the water of dignity and divinity he offers all people. Women who thirst for this water must do like the woman of Sychar.

> Just then his disciples came. They were astonished that he was speaking with a woman, but no one said, "What do you want?" or, "Why are you speaking with her?" Then the woman left her water jar and went back to the city. She said to the people, "Come and see a man who told me everything I have ever done! He cannot be the Messiah, can he?" They left the city and were on their way to him. . . . Many Samaritans from that city believed in him because of the woman's testimony, "He told me everything I have ever done." (John 4:27-30, 39)

She ventures out to the deep well, risks exposure and judgment, exercises her wit, speaks honestly, believes and proclaims the Messiah. She becomes a tributary of God's saving work in the world.

Roughly a generation before John recounts the Samaritan woman's rebirth at Rachel's well and her ministry of witness to her community, Matthew the Gospel writer chronicles Jesus' birth, underscoring the world's desperation for a savior. Like Jeremiah many years earlier, Matthew senses Rachel's lament. In it he hears the cry of a people comfortless after King Herod has killed all the young male children in and around Bethlehem (Matt 2:18).

If we think crucifixion happened only once, we are mistaken both historically and symbolically. Not only was crucifixion the Roman Empire's favored form of public execution, figurative crucifixion happens whenever, wherever the innocent are sacrificed on altars of family disease, institutional power, or political terror for the purposes of social control. Crucifixion's manifold guises include subtler slaughters than Herod's annihilation of baby boys he fears to be the Messiah.

What of the crucifixion of girls? For all the dangers—some self-pursued, some thrust upon me—I confronted before I grew up, many girls never make it to adulthood. Globally, countless girls succumb to grinding poverty, disease, addiction, sex slavery, and death in teenage childbirth. I know great privilege and luck protected me from a terrible end. Through no higher worthiness than that of girls who die before their time, I was granted time to learn God equally envelops in justice and mercy the poor and the rich, the fortunate and the beleaguered, the great men of history and the women whose names are forgotten.

I learned this at church.

Riding the bus home with Ken after we visited a church for my first time on that wet Easter Sunday, I felt both immense relief that the public spectacle of worship was over and a strong desire to try it again someplace else. This ambivalence would take hold in me, fluctuate and evolve and never entirely leave me.

The next Sunday we rode the bus in a different direction. The city church we attended this time was Presbyterian like the first one, but stylistically the congregation was more orderly and restrained, welcoming and warm without quite the human embarrassment of riches we had encountered on Easter.

The preacher, a tall man in a voluminous black robe with velvet stripes on the sleeves, put me at ease because his gentle style belied his imposing physical presence. What's more, he talked about fears and disbelief as though these were acceptable things to bring to church. He read a Bible a story about a man named Thomas, an outsider and a latecomer who, I could tell, would have distrusted at first sight any banner announcing "He Is Risen!" I started to relax in this cream-walled sanctuary where there seemed to be room enough for a great variety of people, including true believers and those like Thomas and me, who had our doubts.

A woman co-led worship wearing a white robe belted with rope at the waist. Unlike the clergyman, she wore no colorful stole around her neck. After a few weeks of attending Sunday worship at this church, we learned that like Ken's mother, this woman was preparing to serve as a Presbyterian minister. As did other women of the congregation, she invited me to attend a churchwomen's book group and a retreat.

When I worked up the courage to show up at the women's homes and spend a weekend with them at a conference center outside the city, I realized how little courage was required. My impressions were confirmed. These Presbyterians, far from antifeminist religious zealots, were smart, good-humored followers of Jesus for whom faith had everything to do with women's self-respect and societal empowerment. Like Jesus with every seeker he ever encountered, they did not ask me where I had been or what I had done in the past, nor pressure me to be other than I was—a young woman unchurched until yesterday. From these women I learned what matters to God is how people live from now on.

During worship one Sunday, I heard Jesus' words, "Take, eat" and "Drink from it, all of you," just before a woman handed me a piece of bread. "All of you" included me. I ate the bread hungrily and washed it down with a swallow of grape juice. Without fully understanding what I had just done, I savored the jelly doughnut aftertaste and the feeling of belonging to the community of God. Later, in the hushed privacy of his office, the pastor told me my having taken Communion was "okay, but generally we baptize people first. Would you like to be baptized?"

All the water I had run my hands through and submerged myself in, all the water in my life—dishwater, poolwater, rainwater, tears—soon ran together one morning. Asked to name my Lord and Savior before the assembled congregation, I declared him to be Jesus Christ. I was a woman at a well. Water fell from the mouth of a pitcher into a font no deeper than a birdbath. The water was sufficient for the sacrament the pastor, the people, and the Holy Spirit used to wet my hair, rinse me down in prayer, and make me theirs. The pastor said I was baptized into Christ's death, remarking that baptism buried me with Jesus. The purpose and effect of this submergence and grave solidarity would be a glory walk with God, the renovation of me.

Meanwhile, I would attend my first church potluck. Ann, the white-robed woman who co-led worship services, was to be ordained to the ministry of Word and Sacrament late one Sunday afternoon amid the congregation I was, to my amazement, a member of now. I still felt like myself, but my renovation, begun in the love of Ken, was well on its way to making me a new person, not only a lover of God and disciple of Jesus, but one who baked broccoli-and-cheddar quiche to share at a church function.

Church is a place where sweets, wholesome savories and coffee may be enjoyed in abundance for free, but are not the main event. Arguably, even the sacramental common loaf of bread and the unfermented grape juice do not comprise the main event for Presbyterians, whose faith is nourished foremost by God's Word read and proclaimed. The Lord's Supper enacts the Word, without the public hearing of which it cannot be rightly shared. But Presbyterian worship can and often does take place without the meal, so rich a feast do Presbyterians find in Holy Scripture.

I don't recall whether we broke the bread of life and drank from the cup of salvation at Ann's ordination. I do recall the psalm Ann selected to be read, which I heard for the first time that afternoon. Its intimate prayer was a part of the Bible and thus belonged to all people. But the psalm told truths about

God and me so deep I scarcely knew they were in me until this public poetry, expressive of profound personal insight and devotion, shocked me into recognizing what always had been true.

> O LORD, you have searched me and known me.
>
> You know when I sit down and when I rise up; you discern my thoughts from far away.
>
> You search out my path and my lying down, and are acquainted with all my ways.
>
> Even before a word is on my tongue, O LORD, you know it completely.
>
> You hem me in, behind and before, and lay your hand upon me.
>
> Such knowledge is too wonderful for me; it is so high that I cannot attain it.
>
> Where can I go from your spirit? Or where can I flee from your presence?
>
> If I ascend to heaven, you are there; if I make my bed in Sheol, you are there.
>
> If I take the wings of the morning and settle at the farthest limits of the sea,
>
> even there your hand shall lead me, and your right hand shall hold me fast.
>
> If I say, "Surely the darkness shall cover me, and the light around me become night,"
>
> even the darkness is not dark to you; the night is as bright as the day,
>
> for darkness is as light to you.
>
> For it was you who formed my inward parts; you knit me together in my mother's womb.
>
> I praise you, for I am fearfully and wonderfully made.
>
> Wonderful are your works; that I know very well.
>
> My frame was not hidden from you, when I was being made in secret,
>
> intricately woven in the depths of the earth.

Your eyes beheld my unformed substance.
In your book were written all the days that were formed
    for me,
when none of them as yet existed.
How weighty to me are your thoughts, O God! How vast is
    the sum of them!
I try to count them—they are more than the sand; I come
    to the end—I am still with you. (Ps 139:1-18)

I appreciated the import of Ann's vocational initiation. Having newly learned to love singing hymns with other Christians, I stood and lifted my voice. I marveled when Ann kneeled (which Presbyterians do rather rarely in public), and the numerous ordained people present laid their hands on her in prayer. But a young woman in the throes of her own spiritual awakening can find it hard to attend wholeheartedly to someone else's big moment. As the service went on, my bones reverberated with scriptural words that told me my life mattered and made blessed sense: "You have searched me and known me. I praise you, for I am fearfully and wonderfully made."

Was I too self-centered? I think not. I was self-conscious to be sure. We come as we are into the presence of the holy and God's beloved people. Jesus came to those who had such pre-existing conditions as wounded spirits and nervous minds. He embodied an invitation unconditioned by any requirement that we shape up before accepting his offer. Gratitude for Christ's wide welcome, not anxiety we don't warrant it, is what motivates people to change for the better.

During the potluck reception that followed the ordination service, I worried I should be different and care more about others than myself. Generosity of spirit is without question the essence of New Testament ethics, as I was learning week by week from listening to my pastor and watching parishioners in action. They volunteered to spend nights awake staffing the homeless shelter housed in the church's basement.

They wrote letters to elected officials, appealing for just and compassionate legislation. Ann was now ordained to ministry, not introspection. They all seemed to have their faith figured out. They knew what to do and apparently spent little time struggling to determine who they were in God's sight.

I seemed to have figured out very little. I was only beginning to read the holy book in which, I was astonished to discover, my own days were written. When, in the midst of the ordination service, I came upon a portion of this Bible that articulated my inmost thoughts and portrayed me as God's exquisitely wrought daughter, the profoundly buried awareness of my real identity was unearthed and thrust upon my consciousness. The force of it all dismantled the hopeless illusions I had long mistaken for reality. My sense not only of myself, but of what it is to be human, was utterly remade by the psalm of the searched and known person. It was, or could be, the prayer of every soul. Chatting, munching quiche and cookies in the church reception hall seemed bizarrely mundane activities for a people beheld in adoration by the Author of their lives.

But then, ordinariness mingled with sublimity is what comprises human spiritual life. For instance, we engage in such animal necessities as feeding, and we manage to turn feeding into a ritual feast. We use the stuff of culture readily at hand (wheat bread, grape juice) to communicate the ineffable. It would take me years to reconcile in my mind the commonplace character of church with the magnificence and mystery toward which church points. But on this evening of Ann's ordination, I neither understood nor needed to. With Ken, I went home happy—for Ann, for others, and for myself, immersed by another inch or two in Christian life.

I can breathe, but the air is orangey with fire, orbs of fire flaring and plummeting above and around me. They endanger and illumine; they could burn me terribly, but by their light I see my upward path and press on. What mountain this is I don't know. I'm climbing it frightened yet fervent to make the ascent. I reach the edges of a high lake. Its water reflects the falling sky-fires. I can hear their gaseous hiss. In the lake stands a young man, submerged to his chest, his eyes firelit. "Remember you're sacred," he tells me.

I dreamed it that night after Ann's ordination and woke up gasping and shaken. The counselor I soon consulted said Carl Jung would have called it a "big dream." Jung borrowed the term from the Elgoni, an East African tribe he visited in 1925. Their shamans, serving as mediators between the spiritual and tangible worlds, dreamed "big" in archetypal symbols, on behalf of the community.

In "Winding Through Big Dreams Are the Threads of Our Lives," (*New York Times*, July 3, 2007) Rebecca Cathcart writes, " 'Back to life' or 'visitation' dreams, as they are known among dream specialists and psychologists, are vivid and memorable dreams of the dead. They are a particularly potent form of what Carl Jung called 'big dreams,' the emotionally vibrant ones we remember for the rest of our lives."

In my big dream it's the dreamer who is summoned back to life. Call her Rae or Rachel; call her by the name of any girl whose vitality has been drowned in shame. She has gone lifeless for years, buried in the water-tomb of unconsciousness, the unlit place where crucial but disallowed knowledge stays submerged until someone exhumes it. The mountain-climb is the journey from the underworld, the fires, forbidden awareness burning for attention, threatening to destroy the one who persists in ignoring them. The boy in the water is the baptized, crucified, and risen One who mediates between earth and heaven, dragging us out of our deadlocks, alerting us to our sacred identity, thrusting us into the hard, holy work of living.

And it was hard work. Hardest for me was the long reckoning with the fact that baptism starts a new life more demanding than the old one. My small undertakings and grand overtures—writing poems, working part-time jobs, and enrolling in graduate school, daily learning to be loved and love faithfully, wedding my life to Ken's in church on an October afternoon—taught me I was being given tremendous gifts of healing, yet I still had in me the hurt girl I had hoped to leave behind in the water. She came with me into the new life. She had been abandoned before, rejected and banished before. If I did again to her what others had done, she would make my days a living hell as no one else could do. After all, she was me, and she knew where the tender nerves were buried.

The same counselor who had classified the big dream startled me with a suggestion: after completing my master's degree in creative writing, enroll in theological seminary. I laughed and protested. I protested, smiled, and sensed he had read a few pages ahead in the book of my life. I had gone to him for help because in my angriest moments I felt God wasn't lifting a finger. All faith in God did was give me someone new to blame for the lingering pain in my soul, which I no longer chose to blot out with reckless behavior (unless you count my having taken out a few student loans).

I was newlywed to a thoughtful, funny man who liked my poetry and the way I looked wearing glasses. We shared a small apartment where faulty wiring meant flipping one of the bathroom light switches turned off the refrigerator. We were in love, and we just didn't flip that switch. Life could scarcely have been better. But even at their best, one's twenties are a thousand novel navigations toward maturity, and the trip is inherently difficult. It's harder for people who didn't internalize crucially early the positive, reliable regard of adult guardians, or learn God's unfailing love is even greater. Under everyday pressures, my choice was to remain a furious youngster, part crying baby, part defiant adolescent, or do the hard work of becoming an adult with adult faith, who trusts God is neither a coddler nor an abandoner but one who abides with us kindly and wisely.

I enrolled in seminary looking for this abiding God. The tricky thing about spiritual seeking is its blindfolded quality. You don't know what you seek. If you did, seeking wouldn't be needed. It is need itself, of the least rational, describable kind, that drives a young woman to the well. She may tell herself it's an everyday errand she's running, it's ordinary water she's after. But the One sought knows better, having drawn her there to be found.

CHAPTER
7

Bible Memory Helps

To preach the Word and teach the people, administer sacraments, and care for souls—these are the tasks of ministry theological seminaries educate would-be pastors to do. I have heard seminaries facetiously referred to as vo-tech schools. The faculty at the urban, exceedingly multicultural seminary I attended expected academic rigor of their students but were also sensitive to the reality that most of us would go on to serve congregations, not teach in universities.

Unlike many of my classmates, I did not have a clear sense of call. I was less motivated by a sense of religious vocation than spiritual quest. I studied in search of the God who had thundered my childhood thoughts, who had seemed to elude my desire for years then instantly accepted the long-delayed prayer from which I emerged a believer at last. As a seminarian I pursued a contemplative agenda that caused me to feel like something of an oddball among the pragmatic Presbyterians. For their part, they could not have been more welcoming. Despite their historic reputation as stern predestinarians (believers that God predestines some people for eternal salvation and others for eternal damnation), the Presbyterians who loved me well throughout my first decade of faith were long on hospitality here and now, short on anxiety about where we might be headed hereafter.

The decade had begun for me with baptism. It later included a period during which, having obtained a two-year seminary degree, I could not imagine practicing the vocational technicalities of pastoral ministry and taught college writing instead. I did deepen my involvement in my church during this time, leading Bible studies and serving as a ruling elder on the session, the congregation's governing board. Meanwhile, I wrote some terrible poems, ambitious, garbled things that strove for literary chic infused with religious gravitas. Journal editors rejected them by the fistful. Despondent, I considered giving up writing altogether. Then on a steaming July day, while I was showering to cool down, inspiration struck. I was given the ambition to write poems not for the readers of rarefied periodicals but for my homies, the folks in the pews. I crafted a collection called *In This Meantime: Poems for Advent and Christmas*, which my church reproduced and distributed among congregants. Here is one of the poems, prompted by Luke's account of shepherds whom angels alert to the Christ child's birth in Bethlehem.

Flocking

The black sky brightens;
the night goes
unspeakably sweet. We retreat
in prayerful terror, to find
ourselves again, ordinary as we were,
but searching
uncountable stars.

Mercy, the new purpose
of the night's labor, is shifting
traditions that have long led us.
We sense the wise innocence of the beasts
whose greasy coats and meat have always
warmed and fed us. Without us,
they'll wander as we do now,
from livelihood, for love.

Starlit, scattered sheaves crackle
under our shoes, the dry flesh
of grain breaking like the ancient
laws in our brains,
as we abandon our fields
and take an amber path
to the city

where one surpassing shudder
has sent forth an impossible child.
We walk in the aftershock, our satchels
laden with the fragrant lards
we were saving for our old age.
Here, the commonplace shimmers.
The image of a mother's blue shawl
now draws us near, now compels us
to slip away quickly;

if we linger in the presence
of such everyday beauty,
we'll believe the world is just this
lovely and enduring, and not turning
toward what is more wonderful
than itself.

Theology Today included the poem among articles and book reviews. A composer of sacred music set it to music that a church choir sang. It comprised my first experience of writing as a Christian vocation that benefits the church through devotional reflection, liturgy, and the public discourse of faith.

Poetry can convey meanings for its writer that more prosaic expressions might obscure. How fitting and telling "Flocking" seems to me now. It is a Christmas poem, of course, biblically based. It also tells my own story of making pilgrimage, undergoing transformation, and claiming a vision that exceeds the personal. A girl (an "impossible child" by some estimates) clipped a prayer from a Christmas card to search for her Savior. She retreated for a long while until a new purpose took hold of her and she could abandon disbelief to follow a path toward a place of new birth. There she glimpsed a woman whose labor had brought forth the life the girl sought not merely for herself but for all creation. She did not understand all she was doing, but she did it in response to a summons. She did not comprehend all she wrote, but she wrote faithfully.

Once I realized mystical, poetic gifts could be put to fruitful use in the church, I made my way back to theological seminary, this time intent on preparing for ordained pastoral ministry. After two more years of study, my first decade of faith culminated in my earning the degree with the name no human being can live up to: Master of Divinity. As I wrote my "ords" (the ordination examinations Presbyterians require candidates for ministry to pass), I wore a small, brightly colored pouch on a string around my neck. The pouch contained several *muñecas quitapenas*, Guatemalan worry dolls I thought of as a "crowd of witnesses," faithful friends to see me through the battery of timed tests.

I now think of the dolls as nutshell Presbyterians, portable symbols of *ecclesia reformata, semper reformanda*, the church reformed and ever being reformed whose women and men graciously included me in their ongoing reformation. This ex-atheist had more God-hunger than church experience, but when I got it into my head to prepare to serve as a church leader, Presbyterians supported my intention with prayers, scholarships, education, encouragement, and a ministry internship opportunity.

During this period Presbyterians in general were attempting to retrieve the spiritual baby their Calvinist forebears had thrown out with the dogmatic bathwater. Marjorie Thompson, Ben Campbell Johnson, and Howard Rice were among Presbyterians who published books in the 1990s to help Protestants practice historically informed Christian spiritualities. These authors responded instructively to people's widespread hunger for a faith consisting as much of experiential relationship with God as cerebral assent to theological tenets. During the same period Anne Lamott and Kathleen Norris emerged as bestselling authors with Presbyterian affiliations. Their books connected personal narrative and Christianity in soulful, hilarious ways relevant to present-day readers, especially women. Yet they carried on a literary tradition as old as St. Augustine, author of *Confessions*, the first-ever spiritual autobiography.

Although my theological seminary's appropriately ministry-centered curriculum has since evolved to include courses on spiritual readings and practices, it largely lacked such offerings while I was a student in the 1990s. Fortunately I was easily able to cross-register for spirituality courses in nearby theological seminaries, including Catholic Theological Union. Between the poems I appended to my Biblical Studies course papers and the prayer-focused classes I found within reach, I fashioned, with the help of an imaginative academic advisor, an unofficial major in spiritual writing.

Nowadays "Best Of" spiritual writing anthologies appear annually and spiritual autobiographies abound. In "God's

Words: The (Unnecessary) Rise of the Spiritual Memoir," reviewer Jess Crispin makes this sweeping complaint: "These past few years . . . have seen a crazy rush on the subject matter, with everyone who has ever thought about religion feeling the need to write about it" (*The Smart Set,* September 24, 2008). Meanwhile, many observers of mainline Christianity fret about denominations' shrinkage and churches' certain demise. A writer of faith may face the vexing problem of making yet one more "unnecessary" contribution to an overloaded literary market, in the service of a dying religion. Why bother?

I bother because I notice myself turning toward what is more wonderful than me. I need to tell the story. A girl as good as dead somehow notices a healer's hand laid on her and gets up. A woman wan from blood loss who notices the fringe of the healer's garment musters just enough nerve to grasp it and be made well. A psalmist, depressive perhaps, insomniac maybe, notices daybreak pushing darkness away and calls the light "my Lord." A moralist noticing the difference between foolishness and wisdom characterizes both of them as women. A woman notices the fortune she stores in an alabaster jar will be worthless until she spills it on one who affirms her humanity. God notices prostitutes, rape victims, infertile and repeatedly married women still bearing in their weary beings the holy love knit into them when they were formed in their mothers' wombs. The world notices when a woman gives birth to its Messiah. The seas swell, the trees burst into green applause. The mountains aspire to lift up all creatures. Among them it's the humans who were fashioned to tell stories. People notice in ourselves the signature of life's Author. In Scripture we discover God and our own precious, numbered days. The urge to recount them, to write our sacred lives, becomes too great to resist. It is necessary.

And it is hazardous. A writer's life is never hers alone, but peopled with relations, friends, and associates who would surely tell a different story and could be wounded by an un-kind account. The most challenging aspect of writing this book I call a cruciform memoir has been recounting some of the parenting I experienced without either prettifying the difficult past or dishonoring my mother and father. Largely in response to their complicated influence on my spiritual development, I became a person who aches for God and is determined to practice honesty, to exercise the voice that is great within. I love my parents as a daughter loves the people of whom she is flesh and bone. This love, involuntary yet dutiful at times and distant at others, is always grounded in gratitude for the life they conceived and called by my name.

Despite my parents' irreligiosity and spiritual wounds, or in part because of these, I grew like an elm seed stuck in the soil under a sidewalk, twisting and groping for sunlight. Mine was not an unusually bitter childhood. If the stories of biblical women and the profusion of present-day spiri-tual memoirs tell us anything, it's that lots of girls have it hard, yet God is good. Hardship prompts some of us to hunt down the Holy One who is there for the finding and following. For memoirists the hunt is retrospective, though if we're honest, rarely nostalgic. Romanticizing history may recapture an idealized image of the Lord who kept our sweet souls while we slept as children, but is unlikely to aid us in awakening to an adult faith. The yearning for just that, a healed and mature relationship with the God who can turn people toward the life beyond us, is evident in these times rife with chronicles of faith.

The cruciform pattern of the faith I chronicle was laid out long before my mother and father conceived me. Cruciform life reaches downward into foundational earth and upward into intangible heights. It opens out at angles parallel to both the daily and the divine, to things below and things above. Cruciform life is lived at multiple levels at once, the mundane and the ethereal cohabiting in a person whose wholeness consists of lively unsolved paradox. I die to live and so do you, patterned as we are on the crucified and risen Christ. Only you can tell the story of your cruciform life. Telling mine faithfully means breaking silences to speak faithfully and disclosing secrets to write truthfully. Telling my story also means giving voice to poetry, the concentrated language of a reminiscent, prayer-insistent mind.

Fatherland

Joe Poževalken is the mythic Lithuanian who lives
under the sidewalk in Chicago near Armitage and
     Damen,
the neighborhood where my father grew up.
Joe is cousin to Mr. Schneepa, the invisible trickster
who lived in my childhood house, stealing single socks
and multiple cookies. Google Joe Poževalken
and you come up with nothing, as though

he doesn't exist. Way to go, Joe. You have flown
successfully under the radar of memory,
absconding with artifacts we
third-generation Lithuanians now have no way of
     retrieving.

You took the i out of Srubas, our surname.
You took the little iron pigs my father played with as
     a boy.
You took his dutiful faith. All that remains is a gray
     portrait:
a somber communicant in knickers with his hand
     on the Bible.
You took the Bible, Joe, and the rosary, and my
     grandmother, Agnes,

whose name meant "pure" and "holy."
Your underworld storehouse must be awfully roomy
to contain all that immigrant trauma and treasure—
seasickness, fear, and midnight evictions,
language, Baltic and chewy as rye bread.
We descendants don't descend if we can help it,
Joe Under-the-Sidewalk. It's too dark down there,
and we have accomplished too much in our America
to bother being Lithuanian. We're white.
We're paper, unsullied by stories of the old country.

Mother Tongue

The words of my mouth,
the notes in my throat,
paragraphs from a black-blooded pen,
percussive alphabet-jazz of the keyboard
under my hands—
these words I live by,
I come by ancestrally.

My maternal grandfather, Puzant Tarpinian,
was able to speak
five languages, but died of secrecy.
He succumbed for slow decades to injuries
from genocide's subtler weapons:
denial, forgetting, and shame.

In 1939, Hitler asked his policy critics,
Who, after all, remembers the Armenians?

I do. I remember the grandfather
I never knew, and the brother, Kaspar,
he never heard from again,

and all the dead Tarpinians,
and the million more martyred Armenians
whose survivors speak a four-thousand-year-old
> *language*
yet taught me everything I know
about never saying what happened.

Puzant's letters to the U.S. State Department,
unanswered, never answered,
are the reasons I bash the keyboard
harder than I have to when I write.
The stories my mother couldn't tell me
because her father couldn't utter them
explain the ellipses in my sense of ancestry
and my penchant for filling unspoken spaces
with talk and ink. I document what I think
to record who I am, to recall who they were,
to question and curse and break silence.
To pray the only way I can, in other words.

On the evening after my ordination to the ministry of Word and Sacrament in the Presbyterian Church (USA), my mother presented me with a beautiful box. She had constructed it from panels of stained and beveled glass soldered together with lead. Under its hinged lid I found stories she could not otherwise tell me. Two heirloom Bibles I had never seen before lay nestled in blue silk wrappings. Their leather covers crumbled with age at the edges. They both were inscribed inside. One had been presented to my mother's maternal grandmother, Jennie, by "her loving husband" in 1889, one hundred years before Ken and I were married. The other, seemingly of comparable vintage, Jennie had presented to my mother on her eleventh birthday.

Inside one of the Bibles I found a dried pressed rose and a paper silhouette identified as that of Margaret Birdsall, my mother's great, great, great grandmother. A yellowed slip stated that Margaret was wedded to John Salmon at the New Windsor Presbyterian Church near Newburgh, New York, on September 4, 1785.

Also tucked in the Bible I found a tattered "Catechism for Infant Classes." Lessons V and VII bore the unmistakable marks of a pencil-wielding toddler. "The Intermediate Catechism," a slender booklet published by the Board of Christian Education of the Presbyterian Church in the United States of America in 1944, was in better shape. Intact but softened by apparent handling was "The Golden Book of Bible Memory Helps." My mother had written her first name in cursive on its cover. Just inside, beneath an artist's rendering of Jesus at about age twelve, the Lord's Prayer appeared in the "debts and debtors" version favored by most Presbyterians.

Earlier on the day my mother gave me the Bibles in the glass box, a Presbyterian congregation had prayed me into my pastoral vocation. I knelt under the weight and heat of their hands, believing I was fairly new to this church tradition. I thought I had no Presbyterian history but the dozen or so years that had passed since my baptism. Now, at a dinner table with my family of origin in the year 2000, I opened a Bible my mother had given me and learned our maternal, Presbyterian ancestry reached back as far as the eighteenth century. Suddenly my sense of myself as a misfit who had departed from the familial flock of agnostics and atheists was replaced by new knowledge of an old, old story. I belonged to a crowd of witnesses, saints whose Christian faith had not endured in my mother beyond her childhood but had taken hold in me. I would keep that faith, and to the people of the church I was now ordained to serve, I would do my best to pass it on.

Passing it on meant pressing on. There was nothing to be gained by regretting faith's lost generation. Parents who decide not to indoctrinate their children in religion often mean to do them the favor of freeing them to make their own choices in adulthood. Christians inclined to criticize mothers and fathers who do not transmit faith to their kids may do well to remember the omission can go the other way. I do not evangelize my parents or siblings.

With those who come to church seeking insight, hope, and courage, I preach the Gospel, pray, and celebrate the sacraments according to my calling. We rise and sing together. We pass the peace of Christ from hand to hand. By these worshipful rituals of assembly, proclamation, praise, taste, and touch, we practice belonging to God and each other. Perhaps we even prove ourselves to be Jesus' brothers and sisters and mothers. A congregation is a family with permeable boundaries. People come; some stay; all eventually go. God abides. In all of this we seek and find our health, our integrity and purpose.

My purpose as a pastor is to foster people's finding what and whom they truly seek. I believe people to be spiritual seekers, however automatic or sluggish their efforts. There is deep in all of us some vision or version of the half-submerged boy with the firelit eyes reminding the dreamer, "You're sacred." You are. We are. From whom would Christ withhold those words? Our longing to hear them relates us to each other and gives me, for one, my life's work of repeating the message. It can be told in sermons, in stories and poems. It can be told, too, to unbelievers, in words and gestures bearing no religious overtones. Often faithfulness practiced, not preached, is the most persuasive kind.

But I prefer to borrow the language of religion, particularly Scripture, because the metaphors blow and swoop, rattle our bones and wake us up. The characters look just like us. If they didn't, we would have closed the book ages ago. We keep opening it, and it keeps opening us to God, who desires us to know ourselves and everyone beloved. That desire drove

Jesus to pursue his magnificent mission until he could finally surrender it to what was more wonderful than his temporal life. The Spirit who carries on his work is the same sigh God released, the same poem God spoke when the time dawned for earth to be born. We are Spirit-borne. I breathe as I write as you breathe as you read, and all beings partake of the Spirit. We come, we conspire with clouds and breezes in prayer, we exchange the love that beholds us, and sooner or later we go, having sensed somehow, if only in dying, our inestimable worth.

"He was put to death in the flesh, but made alive in the spirit, in which also he went and made a proclamation to the spirits in prison" (1 Pet 3:18b-19).

She is the Breath

Ruach, *the ancient Hebrew calls her:*
"Wind." Long before daylight
could tell itself from night, Ruach
hovered, brooding over waters,
whispering the world into being.

She's the Creator's secret-keeper,
and she is a well-kept secret, herself,
hidden in the middle of history, disguised
as surprising coincidence, or mystery,
or descending to earth in the form of a bird
or a flame. Spirit
is one of her names,
and she is the breath
in the Word the world turns toward in winter,
when spring seems an impossible promise,
a comforting fiction at best.

I visited a woman on her deathbed
who sighed and blessed me, then died.
Hers was the next best thing
to a voice from the sky, telling me,
You're my beloved.
I couldn't help myself.
I believed.

I even believed
the outlandish stories of Ruach *the Spirit*
resurrecting Jesus
and teaching him to preach in hell.
Coming to faith was like learning to breathe:
I did it on instinct.
I did it for the life of me.

Mine was one of the imprisoned spirits who heard Jesus preach in the Spirit. I cannot say when I first heard the sermon, but I think it was *in utero*, faint but good words coming through to my developing ears between the clicks of God's knitting needles fashioning my flesh. Because this is how my mind works, Scripture's wild resurrection claims made life-giving sense to me once I finally paid them attention in adulthood. My skepticism was no match for the Bible's poetry. But reasonable doubt keeps some people, like Jesus' friend, Thomas, from believing what they cannot see and touch. Add trauma and its offspring, distrust, to the skeptic's psyche, and the outcome may well be an irreligious person whose security resides in proofs. I have no need, desire, or ability to prove or even preach the Gospel to people dubious of mystery at heart. I am at best a sower of the Word. I cannot soften rock into receptive soil. Given my penchant for Godtalk, I go where I can be heard, and I find family in the fellowship of kindred minds that is the church.

I use a small *c* not only for the word "church" but also for the word "catholic," which describes the all-embracing holy community of Christ. In this I follow the example of the Apostles' Creed, that ancient paragraph of belief I once found myself and others reading in concert on a rainy Easter morning. *I believe.* Ironically, that statement in the first-person singular disabused me of my illusory uniqueness. Over time, as I memorized the Creed and found it speaking my convictions, I also found I could not sustain the misfit status I had imagined to be mine since girlhood. I fit. With a great crowd of witnesses who live for God, believers every one, I fit and I belong.

Belonging is one thing. Leading is another.

As long as there has existed "the holy catholic church" (indeed, since well before the Apostle's Creed codified Christian doctrine in the fourth century), women have belonged in church. We have belonged in liturgical vestments, at tables and altars, in leadership ministries, in pulpits. Needless to say, women's calling to lead, to celebrate and preach still does not find a fit in some churches, including those of denominations that practice women's ordination. This means in the early twenty-first-century church, women continue, to varying and lessening degrees, to be misfits. Misfitting can be preferable to the self-distortion of women that their fitting in might require.

Despite my belonging to the church and my life's fitting perfectly in God's hand, as a clergywoman, as a contemplative and poet, and above all as a follower of Jesus, I am still something of an oddity. I live in a culture that prefers patriarchy, extroversion, prose, and lesser gods than the crucified and risen Christ. I could despair, but I take courage daily from biblical women who had it harder than I, whose outsider status was more forcibly maintained by cultural convention, and whose faith and mettle were tougher than mine may ever have to be. I take heart when I read the ancient Easter story of Mary Magdalene, a getting-up girl if ever there was one.

Early on the first day of the week, while it was still dark, Mary Magdalene came to the tomb and saw that the stone had been removed from the tomb. So she ran and went to Simon Peter and the other disciple, the one whom Jesus loved, and said to them, "They have taken the Lord out of the tomb, and we do not know where they have laid him." Then Peter and the other disciple set out and went toward the tomb. The two were running together, but the other disciple outran Peter and reached the tomb first. He bent down to look in and saw the linen wrappings lying there, but he did not go in. Then Simon Peter came, following him, and went into the tomb. He saw the linen wrappings lying there, and the cloth that had been on Jesus' head, not lying with the linen wrappings but rolled up in a place by itself. Then the other disciple, who reached the tomb first, also went in, and he saw and believed; for as yet they did not understand the scripture, that he must rise from the dead. Then the disciples returned to their homes.

But Mary stood weeping outside the tomb. As she wept, she bent over to look into the tomb; and she saw two angels in white, sitting where the body of Jesus had been lying, one at the head and the other at the feet. They said to her, "Woman, why are you weeping?" She said to them, "They have taken away my Lord, and I do not know where they have laid him." When she had said this, she turned around and saw Jesus standing there, but she did not know that it was Jesus. Jesus said to her, "Woman, why are you weeping? Whom are you looking for?" Supposing him to be the gardener, she said to him, "Sir, if you have carried him away, tell me where you have laid him, and I will take him away." Jesus said to her, "Mary!" She turned and said to him in Hebrew, "Rabbouni!" (which means Teacher). Jesus said to her, "Do not hold on to me, because I have not yet ascended to the Father. But go to my brothers and say to them, 'I am ascending to my Father and your Father, to my God and your God.'" Mary Magdalene went and announced to the disciples, "I have seen the Lord"; and she told them that he had said these things to her. (John 20:1-18)

Magdalene's Guidance for Girls
Whose Time Has Come to Get Up

Rise early. Confront the darkness.
If something looks suspicious, call for backup.
Stay out of needless competition.
Save your strength.
Expect to be questioned.
Believe your eyes.
Grieve. Say what hurts.
Admit you're ignorant (when you are).
Negotiate. Require honesty.
Be prepared to haul away the dead.
Unhand a man who won't be held.
Go. Leave the grave behind.
Get a witness.
Tell the people, "I am ascending."
Teach them everything you know.

Acknowledgments

Ken S. McAllister, to whom my heart forever belongs, is the best person ever to happen to me or my writing. Thank you for loving and cheering me on every day, and for reading this manuscript.

The Licona/Lee family fed Ken and me with wonderful food and friendship many times during the writing of this book. Thank you, Jamie and Adela, for reading the manuscript, and bless you, Sophia, Aida, and Grannie.

Others who fortified my spirit and upheld my heart while I wrote include the dear congregation and staff of Mountain Shadows Presbyterian Church; my colleagues and friends in Presbytery de Cristo, especially the Revs. Ellen Dawson and Stuart Taylor; Jean Bronson, who gave me continuing affection and summer writing quarters; the Revs. Brett and Alex Hendrickson, great and faithful friends whose kids, Thomas, Lily, and David honor us with the names Uncle Kenny and Auntie Rachel; good-humored, caring women of prayer: Cassi Fraley, Patricia Casey, Rev. Becky Chamberlin, Barbara Gray, Mary Ann Miya, and Jan Britt.

The people of Liturgical Press are gracious, dedicated and smart. Thank you, Hans Christoffersen, for your encouragement and an invigorating deadline.

Blessings, also, on Mary Stommes, Trish Vanni, Colleen Stiller, Barry Hudock, Stephanie Nix, Ann Blattner, and Peter Dwyer.

Finally, to Ken again, and to the spirited family into which I married: my love.